EXCEPTIONAL ENTREPRENEURIAL WOMEN

Exceptional Entrepreneurial Women

Strategies for Success

Russel R. Taylor

Foreword by Arthur Lipper III

New York
Westport, Connecticut
London

Library of Congress Cataloging-in-Publication Data

Taylor, Russel R.
  Exceptional entrepreneurial women : strategies for success /
Russel R. Taylor; foreword by Arthur Lipper III.
    p. cm.
  Bibliography: p.
  Includes index.
  ISBN 0–275–93107–2 (pbk. : alk. paper)
    1. Women in business—United States—Biography.
  2. Entrepreneurship—United States—Case studies. I. Title.
HD6072.6.U5T39   1988b
338'.04'0922—dc19
[B]   88-15157

A hardcover edition of *Exceptional Entrepreneurial Women: Strategies for Success*
is available from the Quorum Books division of Greenwood Press, Inc.
(ISBN: 0–89930–384–6).

Library of Congress Catalog Card Number: 88-15157
ISBN: 0-275-93107-2

First published 1988

Paperback edition 1988

Praeger Publishers, One Madison Avenue, New York, NY 10010
A division of Greenwood Press, Inc.

Printed in the United States of America

The paper used in this book complies with the
Permanent Paper Standard issued by the National
Information Standards Organization (Z39.48–1984).

10 9 8 7 6 5 4 3 2 1

Copyright Acknowledgment

The author and publisher gratefully acknowledge the following for granting
permission to reprint:

Illustration from *The Woman Entrepreneur* by Robert D. Hisrich and Candida
G. Brush is reproduced with permission of the authors and Lexington Books,
D. C. Heath and Company. Copyright © 1986 by D. C. Heath and Company.

To the two Deborahs in my life,
and Claire, Tarek, and Karim

CONTENTS

FOREWORD

Men and women are different. This element of wisdom or sophistry, depending upon perspective and experience, is my net conclusion from reading *Exceptional Entrepreneurial Women—Strategies For Success*.

Mine is a masculine perspective. I like women and am surrounded by them. My closest business associate is a woman with whom I've enjoyed a constructive relationship for twenty-nine years. My wife of twenty-six years is my active partner and manages a number of commercial activities. I know that a woman must, in most cases, be better equipped than a man to make the same progress within our society. I do not believe that will change. *Venture* magazine has a male-dominated circulation. Ninety-five percent of our 450,000 paid subscribers are men and 78% are owners or partners in their businesses. The average household income of a *Venture* subscriber is $122,000 and the average net worth $793,000. Most of the members of *Venture*'s Association of Venture Founders (AVF) are male. It is my close association with *Venture* and AVF that provides me with the authority to discuss entrepreneurs, particularly successful entrepreneurs, as a group.

With men there is a lust, a sex drive, a power need associated with the building of a business. Certainly the business becomes an additional if not a replacement family for male entrepreneurs. They have a passion to play the game of business. Certainly, they want, and in most cases have to, make money. However, it is not the making of a good or even truly superior living that drives male entrepreneurs. They build and grow because that is what they must do. They are compulsive and compelled. They tend to be faithful to their spouses because they are really infatuated with, and held captive by, their businesses.

Male entrepreneurs seek recognition and frequently had a childhood perception of themselves as being different from their peers. That difference could have been in height, weight, intellect, outlook, or some other attribute. The important thing is that they accepted the difference rather than trying to assimilate, even were that possible. Also, male entrepreneurs probably tended to play sports in which they were either alone, as in tennis or skiing, or in a position to have made a real difference in the outcome of the event. I am convinced that we can identify those youngsters having entrepreneurial tendencies well before they reach junior high school age.

In trying to understand why successful women entrepreneurs seem so different from their male counterparts, one should consider the early traditional training of most girls versus boys, even in this country. A girl is or was taught or given to understand that she should be perfect and "nice to Daddy." After all, Daddy is the source, in most family situations, of funding. A girl therefore becomes burdened with a perception of a typical parental expectation that she will do things "right" and not make mistakes. Perhaps the early training of girls had changed and the expectations that influenced the attitudes and personalities of today's mature woman are different now. I hope so. Remember that "executives do things right, while entrepreneurs do the right thing." Boys, on the other hand, are indoctrinated with their sense of values primarily through the playing of sports. Therefore, they know that in each game there will be a winner and a loser and that it is okay to lose as long as one played hard and well. If there were but a single thing parents could do to help a child who has entrepreneurial tendencies develop into a successful entrepreneur, it would be to let the youngster know it is all right to fail and that a person's worth is not measured by the results of an inning or quarter, but rather by the score that can be calculated only at the end of the game of life.

Although about 35 percent of the students taking entrepreneurship education classes in the more than 300 colleges offering some form of "profit education" are women, females make up a much smaller part of the new-business-starting, entrepreneurial body. One of the reasons for this fact is that it is so much more difficult for a woman to gain control over other people's assets, either in the form of investment or in loans, than for a man under similar circumstances. For many, successful entrepreneuring is an exercise in the successful use of leverage. It is a fact of life that most start-up businesses just do not have the funds necessary to achieve their projections. Another reason for the less-than-could-be participation of women in the hundreds of thousands of new businesses started every year is the much harsher penalty society imposes on a woman running a business that fails to achieve the desired results. For a man it is so much easier, as it is generally believed that he "can always come back again in another company." Many seem to take the view that the woman who failed in business did so because she shouldn't have been there in the first place. It is wrong, unfair and stupid . . . but nevertheless a prevalent and continuing prejudice.

This foreword is addressed to those women, of all ages, who are considering starting a business and who have acquired this book in order to learn about truly successful women entrepreneurs and the strategies employed. My advice to you is *not* to start a business alone. Rather, find a mentor or a partner who has had the experience of previously starting a successful business and join forces in some way. They don't award medals for doing it alone. They do penalize those who fail. Why not take along on your journey a pathfinder, someone who has done it before? By all means embrace the entrepreneurial dream of self-determination and do what is necessary to own a business. However, recognize that most of your efforts, certainly in the early stages of the business, are going to be to earn enough money to pay landlords, lenders and the other asset owners for whom most in business really work.

Last, and most important, I have never known a business person who didn't agree that they'd have been much better off if they had terminated a disappointing business earlier than they did. Owning and operating a business is a bit like the game of backgammon in that it is a matter of constant assessment and re-evaluation. At such time as the odds favor redirecting the employment of one's assets and resources, a fear of having to admit having been wrong or of making a mistake should not be an impediment to taking salvaging, corrective action. If more entrepreneurs and private company investors or "angels"–and the two are very much the same, as they are both dealing with their personal resources–were to invest using more consideration and therefore more slowly, and exit from declining situations more quickly, they would die richer.

Russ Taylor is to be congratulated for his efforts to assist young women having an interest in becoming entrepreneurs. However, it is my hope that he spends some time also exposing the darker sides of business ownership, rather than just the winners' circle, which is what this book really describes and which it could have been entitled. Owning a business is not for everyone any more than all want to be or should be captains of ships. For those who succeed, the experience is just wonderful. The employer has an ability to impact positively the lives of employees as the entrepreneur's family grows. "Am I working for them or they for me?" is a fair question most business owner-employers at one time or another ask themselves. My answer is "probably *both*, and what difference does it make if it is working?"

Arthur Lipper III

PREFACE

At the age of eleven, thanks to my father, I acquired the entrepreneurial spirit.

My dad did not believe in giving allowances to his children and so provided my brother and me with a list of chores for which we were paid "fees." Mowing the lawn, raking leaves, shoveling snow, washing the family car, pressing one of his two suits, each carried a credit of twenty-five cents. Then, in order to encourage our accumulation of wealth, he required us at each month-end to submit a statement of earnings for that month, whereupon he provided a "bonus" of twenty-five cents for each dollar earned from sources both inside and outside the home. With funds thus derived from domestic chores, plus my newspaper route, and commissions earned by selling magazine subscriptions door-to-door in the small Canadian city where we lived, by my twelfth birthday I was able to amass a fortune of $100. My father suggested that I invest this sum in the shares of a copper-mining company trading on the Toronto Stock Exchange. A stockbroker neighbor gave me the positive assurance that this investment would make me rich!

For Christmas of 1928 I received an unusual present from a relative. It was a hand-operating printing press capable of printing personal stationery and business cards. It came with an assortment of types and inks in various colors. Now I was really in business, soliciting friends and neighbors for orders at prices below what they would have to pay at a local printing shop. Monthly sales from the business soon soared to $15 a month, with my expenses limited to the purchase of blank paper and envelopes. In consequence, an unexpected problem was created for my father when I submitted monthly statements demonstrating total earnings averaging $20 a month, which required him to shell out $5 for each $20 earned. The "pinch" was somewhat traumatic for him, so he objected to my claims of earnings, arguing that my expense records should include the cost of ink used and that there should be an expense charge for "depreciation" of the equipment which were the "fixed assets" of my business.

Most kids of the age of twelve have no knowledge of such terms as "gross profit," "net profit," let alone "depreciation of fixed assets," but since big money was involved here I soon learned about them, and more. Dad always dealt with everyone in the spirit of fair play in all his dealings, and because I was adamant in my claim that there should not be a charge against sales for the ink and "depreciation," he suggested we present the case for "arbitration" before a family acquaintance who was a professional accountant. We went together before the arbitrator—each of us stating our individual claims—and, after careful consideration, the arbitrator decided in my favor due entirely to the fact that I had received the equipment, as well as a large supply of ink, as a *gift*, and therefore could carry both on my books of account as zero. Thus, there should indeed not be a charge for depreciation or the utilized ink in my statement of earnings. I gloated over my victory!

This was in October of 1929, the time of the great crash in the stock market. My father was heavily invested at the time and was literally wiped out as a result of the precipitous decline in stock values. My own investment in the copper mine shares was all but worthless and my family, like many others of that time, embarked upon hard times. The company where my father was employed closed its local branch facility and transferred him—at a greatly reduced salary—to a plant in another city where he took up residence in the local YMCA. My mother became depressed and had what was then labeled a "nervous breakdown," and after several months of hospitalization, she went to live with one of her sisters who had married into considerable wealth. My brother had started his freshman year at McGill University in Montreal and was able to obtain room and board with relatives living there. I moved in with an aunt and uncle in a nearby town and continued in high school, but worked after school and on Saturdays in my uncle's drugstore.

In retrospect, I did not see these years as hard times, for I had a roof overhead, three meals a day, people who cared for me, and was earning enough spending money to take my high school sweetheart to Friday night movies. I also began to think about my future and dreamed that someday I would have my own business and make lots of money. But first, I needed a college education. I was able to obtain a full-tuition scholarship to the University of Toronto where I spent four delightful years and graduated in 1938, with a latent desire to return, someday, to campus life.

Twenty-three years later, with a bank loan of $25,000 that was guaranteed by a wealthy friend and college classmate, Russel Taylor, Inc. was launched. The company, with only a few set-backs, grew and flourished—so much so that one of the conglomerates of the 1960s acquisitions era acquired it in exchange for several millions of dollars worth of its stock, thus enabling me subsequently to choose my second career as an academic.

Teaching business subjects in the School of Arts and Sciences at the College of New Rochelle—where only women are enrolled—has enabled me to discern the incredible discrimination of past years against women's upward mobility on the corporate executive ladder. Also, having been imbued at an early age with the entrepreneurial spirit, I have become fascinated with the current mounting trend toward a display of successful entrepreneurship among the ranks of women. That fascination has motivated me to write this book.

ACKNOWLEDGMENTS

I wish to give special thanks to all of the subject women and others whom I have interviewed for this book. Entrepreneurs are extraordinarily busy folks and all of them gave me their valuable time to assist in my research. I am especially grateful to my colleague, Dr. Joan Carson, Professor of English at the College of New Rochelle, for her encouragement and critique of the manuscript. Particular thanks go to Vera Mezzaucella for typing the manuscript and providing her secretarial service in the voluminous correspondence that was necessary in pulling the project together.

Part I

PROFILES

1

INTRODUCTION

Entrepreneurship appears to be a subject whose time has come for new study. The *Encyclopedia of Entrepreneurship*, published in 1982, attempted to distill all the literature that had theretofore evolved on the subject.[1] It reported on several thousand books and articles on entrepreneurship, and concluded that much more research is needed, especially on the process of entrepreneurship itself. The editors decried the fact that our understanding of what kindles the spark that flames into new ventures, of what factors cause some to succeed while others falter, and of what environmental conditions promote or discourage risk taking, is limited. The editors also pointed out that most studies have concentrated on the male entrepreneur and, although it is believed that about one-quarter of all new business formations are created by women, little research effort has focused solely on women entrepreneurs.

An exception to this is a joint research project conducted by Robert Hisrich of the University of Tulsa and Candida Brush of Boston College, published in 1985.[2] Their work included a survey of 468 women entrepreneurs responding to 1,000 mailed questionnaires. Thirty-five of the respondents were selected for an interview either in person or by telephone. Among their findings were that "the typical woman entrepreneur is the first-born child of middle-class parents—a self-employed father and a mother who does not work outside the home. After obtaining a liberal arts degree, she marries, has children and works as a teacher, administrator, or secretary. Her first business venture in a service area begins when she is thirty-five, with her biggest problems being finance, credit, and lack of business training."[3] My research of the careers of the exceptionally successful entrepreneurial women profiled in this book does not tend to support all of the Hisrich and Brush findings.

Peter Drucker, the prolific author on business subjects, published in 1985 an important book on the subject of *Innovation and Entrepreneurship*.[4] In his conclusions, Drucker suggested that the current emergence of America as an *entrepreneurial society* may be a major turning point in our history, arguing that it is the exploitation of innovative ideas by America's entrepreneurs—both male and female—and the consequent process of creating new business that has propelled the U.S. work force to the highest numerical level in its history. This remarkable phenomenon has created forty million new jobs since the late 1960s.[5] It is significant to point out that the new enterprises founded by the fifteen women entrepreneurs whose careers are outlined in this book have created new jobs for approximately 220,000 people.

One of the purposes of my research has been to determine what personal characteristics seem not only to be common but apparently necessary for all of them to have reached their exceptional levels of achievement. This was the guiding factor in my selection of each subject to be profiled in this book. All of them meet the criteria I established in selecting them, namely:

1. Each is well known in her industry.
2. Each started her own business or acquired businesses with her own resources.
3. Each of their businesses exceeds $10 million in annual sales.

All of them, in achieving success, have inspired my selection of the book's title. They are the kind who did not sit on their haunches waiting for something to happen. Indeed, all are the kind who *make things happen*.

Good research requires the use of sample surveys. The larger the sample, the better the results. Thus, a selected sample of fifteen would not necessarily be characteristic of most women entrepreneurs in America, and any standard test for statistical significance in such a small sample would not be meaningful. In selecting the candidates to be interviewed, I sought to maximize diversity as best I could. The ages of my subjects range from thirty to eighty. Industries represented by these entrepreneurs include food, cosmetics, toys, advertising, real estate brokerage, women's apparel, finance, marketing research, travel agencies, radio and TV broadcasting, retail stores, and mail-order sales. Nevertheless, there is a framework, or at least a thread of continuity and commonality, among all of the subjects I have profiled.

It is reported that women are starting new enterprises in the United States at more than three times the rate of men, yet there is an almost complete void in the literature—other than magazine articles with biographical sketches of prominent women who have succeeded in their individual activities.

Shelves of bookstores are filled with titles directed toward women on how to achieve success in a man's world. Recently, there has appeared a limited number of volumes on tips and suggestions for women starting their own businesses. One of these, *The Self-Employed Woman* by Jeanette Scollard, attempts to analyze all the logical bases to be covered by a woman about to start her own business.[6] Two national monthly publications, *Savvy* and *Working Woman*, provide a consistent focus on the activities, opportunities, and areas of interest for executive women. *Venture* which boasts a monthly circulation of 450,000 concentrates on matters of interest to all entrepreneurial business owners and investors. *Inc.* and *Entrepreneur* also cater to some of the same markets.

Historically, America's best-known women entrepreneurs tended to concentrate their activities in the apparel, cosmetics, and food-processing fields. Names like Helena Rubinstein, Elizabeth Arden, and Anne Klein are familiar to most—although all three are deceased. Lane Bryant, also deceased, founded the world's largest apparel retail-store chain specializing in sizes to fit large and tall women, and created an innovation that is still going strong. The name of the late Margaret Rudkin may not be familiar to most readers, yet she was the entrepreneur who started Pepperidge Farm (now a division of Campbell Soup Company) after discovering that the high-quality bread baked in her own kitchen was literally gobbled up by fellow commuters of her stockbroker husband as he rode daily from Connecticut to New York on the New Haven Railroad during the early 1930s.

Funk and Wagnall's dictionary defines an 'entrepreneur' as "one who undertakes to start and conduct an enterprise or business, assuming full control and risk." David McClelland, a prolific writer on managerial motivation in business, a former professor at Harvard University, and now a private consultant, is less restrictive, claiming that an innovative manager who has decision-making responsibility is as much an entrepreneur as the owner of a business.[7] Peter Drucker, probably the most prolific writer on management subjects in America today, proclaims that one of the keys to successful executive management lies in creating and fostering the *entrepreneurial spirit* in all of one's subordinates.[8]

In recent years, *intrapreneurship*, a new word, has evolved in the literature of management,. It refers to the practice of well-known corporations, including IBM, 3M Corporation, Hewlett-Packard and many others, permitting their own employees with creative new product concepts to develop them on company time, and to share in the rewards of their endeavors, sometimes through subsidiary corporations formed for the purpose of rewarding the innovators with equity participation, thus stemming the departures of would-be entrepreneurs from their employers in order to establish their own businesses. Gifford Pinchot has recently published a book entitled *Intrapreneuring*.[9]

Robert Brockhaus, Professor of Management and director of the Small Business Institute at St. Louis University, states that the factors associated with the decision to become an entrepreneur can be divided into three categories: psychological influences upon the individual, effects of previous experiences (especially previous jobs), and personal characteristics.[10] The interviews conducted by the author with the fifteen women in this study and reported in the following chapters tend to support Brockhaus's conclusions.

Researchers on entrepreneurship have discovered that modern entrepreneurs tend to differ from their forebears; they cite changes in the dynamics of the U.S. economy that require them to be more aware of the behavioral responses of their subordinates as their businesses grow and flourish, less authoritarian in their managerial processes, more willing to accept change and to use new technological advances particularly in the area of computers. David McClelland ascribes the "high need for achievement" as being characteristic of the entrepreneur, and other researchers have published data indicating that this need is no different among the new breed of entrepreneurs than has been found among some modern corporate managers."[11]

Much has been written about *role models* and *mentors* as having been a guiding influence on entrepreneurial inspiration. Some writers have stated that acquaintances and family members provide the principal role models, and that an unusually high percentage of entrepreneurs had fathers who were themselves entrepreneurs. The research involved in this book does not tend to confirm that finding.

Existing studies report that entrepreneurs tend to be better educated than the general population but *less so* than successful managers. There appears to be a wide variation in the formal education of entrepreneurs and, with the exception of those in highly technical industries, a large majority of them are not college graduates, as is the case with eight of the fifteen women interviewed in this study. Some exhibit an extraordinary knowledge concerning the liberal arts and all have found ways of acquiring knowledge and skills by experience and self-teaching.

Social and ethnic variables that are associated with entrepreneurs indicate that many of them perceived themselves as "outsiders" who could survive only by performing roles considered to be outside or beneath the domain of established groups. This appears to be particularly true in the cases of many women entrepreneurs. As Lois Wyse of Wyse Advertising states it: "They tend to fight for their own identity and, in the process, become strong. They get a kind of courage that comes from early success and even *stamina* to try again when failure occurs."[12] The research on entrepreneurs in general indicates that Jews and Lebanese and, in a limited way, Chinese-Americans, tend to fall into this group. More recently, certain refugee groups, notably Cubans, Koreans, and Vietnamese, are found among the growing number of entrepreneurs in America during the past decade.[13]

Environmental influences on entrepreneur stimulation are cited throughout the literature. For example, Silicon Valley in California and Route 128 around Boston have become popularized in U.S. business literature as the launching grounds for entrepreneurs in the high-tech fields, due mainly to specific environmental factors. Noted here are the availability of venture capital, highly skilled labor, access to suppliers, customers, and new markets, proximity to colleges and universities with research labs, and good living conditions. These factors appear to have influenced the entrepreneurial careers of entrepreneurs like Maryles Casto of Casto Travel in California, profiled in this book.

A great deal of literature is currently evolving on the subject of *intuition* in decision making. Intuition, once maligned as a purely "feminine" way of thinking, is now thought to be a powerful tool for making creative decisions.[14] Many writers on the subject of intuitive thinking refer to the scientific knowledge that the right side of the brain—the intuitive, imaginative hemisphere—is as important in decision making as the left hemisphere, which is known to be the logical, rational half. In a recent publication, *The Intuitive Manager*, Roy Rowan explains how the intuitive mind organizes previous impressions, past encounters, and relationships into a path that is used by many prominent decision-makers.[15] He cites the flash of intuition or the "Eureka Factor" as being the key element in many great discoveries and creative processes from the ancient days of Archimedes, the Greek physicist, to the transformation of Bendel's fashion store by Geraldine Stutz, reviewed in a subsequent chapter of this book. A keen intuition or "gut instinct" appears to be pervasive among successful entrepreneurs. Could it be that women are more gifted in the intuitive domain than men?

NOTES

1. C. A. Kent, D. L. Sexton, and K. H. Vesper, eds., *Encyclopedia of Entrepreneurship* (Englewood Cliffs, N.J.: Prentice-Hall, 1982).

2. Robert D. Hisrich and Candida G. Brush, *The Woman Entrepreneur* (Lexington, Mass.: Lexington Books, 1985).

3. Ibid., p. 14.

4. Peter Drucker, *Innovation and Entrepreneurship*, (New York: Harper & Row, 1985).

5. Ibid., p. 3.

6. Jeanette R. Scollard, *The Self-Employed Woman* (New York: Simon & Schuster, 1985).

7. *Encyclopedia of Entrepreneurship*, p. 75.

8. Peter Drucker, *Management* (New York: Harper & Row 1974), p. 45.

9. Gifford Pinchot, *Intrapreneuring* (New York: Harper & Row, 1985).

10. *Encyclopedia of Entrepreneurship*, p. 85.

11. Ibid., p. 47.

12. Personal interview with Lois Wyse, April 1986.

13. *Encyclopedia of Entrepreneurship*, p. 12.

14. Kim Wiley, "Gut Instincts," *Savvy*, May 1986, p. 79.

15. Roy Rowan, *The Intuitive Manager*, (Boston: Little, Brown & Co., 1986).

2

LOIS WYSE

She Writes Books on the Side

Lois Wyse

Typical of many successful entrepreneurs, Lois Wyse left school and went to work at the age of seventeen. A gifted writer, Lois got her first job as a reporter for the *Cleveland* (Ohio) *Press*. Her parents—Ray and Rose Wohlgemuth—lived modestly in a middle-class area of Cleveland, and were not entirely enchanted when she eloped with Marc Wyse, a local jock who had been her high school sweetheart.

Together they started a small mail-order business which later failed, and Lois went to work in the advertising department of The Higbee Company, a leading Cleveland department store. A talented and creative copywriter, she rose to the position of advertising director of the store. In 1961, at the age of thirty-five, she left Higbee's, and with $6,000 borrowed from her father, she and Marc Wyse started Wyse Advertising. Lois's years with Higbee's not only honed her advertising executive talents, but brought her into touch with many businesses throughout Ohio. In consequence, the company flourished to become one of Cleveland's foremost ad agencies and the Wyses grew into positions of leadership in the community. Lois managed to spark the agency with an uncanny ability to recruit clients with her charm, wit, and talent for words. Even though Lois had departed from Higbee's as its advertising director, the Wyse agency retained the store as a client and Lois became the first woman to be elected to Higbee's board of directors. Following this appointment, she became a board member of Consolidated Natural Gas Company in Pittsburgh, the parent company of its Cleveland subsidiary, East Ohio Natural Gas Company.

The marriage of Lois and Marc Wyse was considered to be "made in heaven"—they had two children, became prominent in the Cleveland community, and built a thriving agency business which expanded to a New York City branch in 1970. Lois found time to pursue her love for writing, and during the years 1963 to 1983 managed to publish forty-seven books. Two of these, *The Rosemary Touch* and *Kiss, Inc.* were sexy novels about men and women in business and sold in the several thousands.

Kiss, Inc. was a novel about a cosmetics tycoon and is said to be a reflection of the life of the late Charles Revson, co-founder of Revlon Cosmetics. *Lovetalk*, written in 1973, is a touching collection of poems in blank verse that reflect the richness and warmth of a happy marital relationship. The final line of the foreword to the book is "And for the rest of my life, I will love you."

In 1982 something happened to the "made-in-heaven" marriage and the Wyses were divorced. Lois settled in New York and later married Lee Gruber, the producer, yet she still remains Marc's partner in Wyse Advertising. Among the clients of that agency are: Stearns & Foster Mattresses, Stroh's Beer, Blue Cross and Blue Shield, Sherwin-Williams Paints, and Stauffer Hotels.

Lois Wyse's talent and creative ability are seen in the body copy and headlines of her clients' advertising. Indicative of this is the well-known caption of Smuckers (jams and jellies) ads—"With a Name Like Smuckers—You've Got to be Good!"

Lois Wyse has a clear and definite view regarding what propels a person to become an entrepreneur. "All entrepreneurs are *outsiders*," says Wyse. "They are not former prom queens or football captains. Those people get absorbed into *corporate* life." Pressed into defining the "outsider," Wyse sees him or her as thinking that they "don't belong" and perceive themselves as "not as smart as others." "Fighting for their own identity, they strive harder and become strong and even develop a stamina to try again when they fail to achieve previously defined goals; so they press on and never give up."

Wyse expresses a skeptical and pessimistic view on opportunities for women in the higher echelons of corporate life. Although serving on the boards of directors of several corporations, she sees women appointees to boards as fulfilling "token" roles. "You'll see a woman in the White House before you will see one as the chief executive of General Motors," claims Wyse. "Women will continue to be prominent in middle and occasionally in upper management—where they have to be better than men—but they get squeezed out at the top." Asked what she meant by the statement "better than men," Wyse retorts that "women are actually smarter than men, because they *listen* more than men. Because of the traditional discrimination against women in management, women must *bend down* not *reach up* in order to open doors."

All the above is the basis for shaping the motivation of the entrepreneurial woman—the *outsider* in Wyse's perception—to start her own enterprise. When pushed further to obtain her profile of the elements common to successful entrepreneurial women, Wyse cites eight components:

1. A high degree of self-confidence
2. Integrity
3. Social charm
4. Articulate
5. Willingness to take risks
6. Immense curiosity
7. Ability to think clearly
8. Keen intuition

In the author's opinion, the above components obtained in his interview with Lois Wyse represent a perfect self-analysis and profile of the subject herself.

3

LILLIAN VERNON KATZ

Queen Mother of Mail Order

Lillian Vernon Katz

In February 1986, the Gannett newspaper chain presented to Lillian Katz its annual Business Leadership award—the first woman so honored in the history of this award. Gannett Westchester publisher, Louis A. Weill, called Lillian Katz a "business woman who embodies the best in entrepreneurial spirit." Most Americans know little of Lillian Katz, but many readily recognize her firm, Lillian Vernon, a mail-order company specializing in gifts, personal and home accessories, toys, gourmet items, housewares, and stationery, with annual sales in excess of $125 million.

Lillian Vernon Corporation sends out 103 million catalogues in 12 seasonal and specialized editions featuring up to 850 individual products, mainly imported from thirty-three countries of the world. The company's mailing list of 9,000,000 names is carefully maintained to record such items as purchase history and in-depth demographic analysis which identifies that 97 percent of Lillian Vernon's customers are women, averaging thirty-eight years of age from households with incomes of over $44,000 a year. Over 65 percent of its customers are employed outside the home. The company's facilities, located in four communities in Westchester County, New York, and Virginia Beach, Virginia, house a work force of 1,000 employees.

Lillian Menasche Katz was born in 1927 in Leipzig, Germany, the second child of well-to-do Jewish parents whose world of affluence disintegrated with the onset of Hitler's Nazi regime. In 1933 the family moved to Holland. When the clouds of World War II began to gather in 1937, and foreseeing a crisis for European Jewry, the family moved to New York where Lillian went to high school and later attended New York University. Her father's business—ladies' lingerie— had been a great success in Europe, and in America, he started a zipper manufacturing company. Plagued with the metal shortages characteristic of wartime, his company had to be content with reconditioning old zippers. Lillian worked after school, alternating between ushering in a movie house and clerking in a candy store. Katz describes her teenage social life in terms of being a kind of "wallflower." Although she was elected treasurer of her high school class, she hated figures—an emotion she struggles with to this day. "I wasn't a prom queen or captain of any teams but I did date a lot until the war came on and all the young men went into the armed services. This may have motivated my first marriage which was far from brilliant," Lillian relates. "I dropped out of college after my sophomore year to get married. My husband, Sam Hochberg, was making $75 per week, and we lived in a tiny apartment in Mount Vernon, New York—and I was pregnant." A desire for an above-average lifestyle, generated from the affluent childhood life of her family in Europe, motivated Lillian to look for some way of making additional money. Her father then operated a small leather goods manufacturing company. With a child coming, Lillian decided she needed a business she could conduct right out of her own kitchen, so with $2,000 of wedding gift money, she bought two items from her father's inventory—a handbag, which she redesigned by adding a small flap, and a belt—both suitable for personalized monogramming. She then took a mail-order advertisement in the September 1951 issue of *Seventeen*, which cost her $495. The unbelievable value of the return orders totaled $16,000. Lillian poured all her profits back into her growing business by taking out more ads and purchasing more handbags and belts. Her business quickly developed into a multimagazine advertising program, and later into a catalog. Dissatisfied with the usual market offerings, Lillian began designing her own items and Vernon Products (named after the town of Mt. Vernon) was born.

Soon the company was engaged in both mail order and in manufacturing custom product containers for firms like Max Factor, Elizabeth Arden, Avon, and Revlon. In 1965 Lillian Vernon Corporation was formed for mail-order sales exclusively. That enterprise has experienced a sales growth, with only one or two setbacks, that have propelled it to its current level of over $125 million in annual sales, and still growing at 10 percent a year.

The company continues to bear the stamp of Lillian Katz's philosophy which stresses the belief that when a customer buys by mail, a feeling of trust is conveyed that must not be betrayed. Her catalogs have a distinct personality with every item selected as though for herself—as indeed they are. Her shopping trips throughout the world engage sixteen weeks of the year, but even when she's on the other side of the globe, she keeps in constant touch with the home office to know what's going on.

At a recent Junior Achievement Awards banquet, she articulated her own two cardinal rules for starting one's own business:

1. Pay as you go
2. Live like a pauper

A visit to her apartment in New York and to her million-dollar weekend retreat in Greenwich, Connecticut would tend to belie her own rules. Lillian Katz did indeed live like a comparative pauper until her business flourished, and the balance sheet of her company still reflects the "pay-as-you-go" rule as she personally watches all expenses.

Asked to give her views on the keys to success in building a business from scratch, Lillian Katz claims that success is not achieved easily but that there are four necessary ingredients:

1. Objectivity
2. Need for achievement
3. Dedication
4. Developing one's *instincts* and learning to trust them

Lillian Katz is one of those entrepreneurs who still finds it hard to let go. "I know every item in my catalogs and I'm one of the few in the firm who seems to be able to determine where each item should be positioned (putting an item in the right-hand top corners of the catalog can mean an extra half-million dollar response). I'm never bored, unhappy, or lonely. My work fills in my time and I'm dedicated to the creative side of my business." Katz has only two regrets in reviewing her brilliant career. "I wish I'd taken more vacations; I also wish I'd taken one of those advanced business courses at Harvard." Like many creative people, Lillian Katz has always been intimidated by balance sheets and other financial statements. "One of my controllers taught me how to read a balance sheet. I'm good at it now—but sorry I didn't learn it sooner."

Katz, like many other successful entrepreneurs whose careers are reviewed in this book, claims to be good at handling crises. Her business in 1984 got into trouble because of too-rapid growth. A brand-new computer system that failed to produce the hoped-for results, coupled with a record Christmas season resulted in a difficult surplus inventory problem that put the company in deep trouble. "There was no question in my mind that I wouldn't pull out with glory." Lillian Katz faced the crisis by methodically cutting back on spending, laying off 10 percent of the employees, and moving her excess inventory with a liquidation sale directly to the public.

In October 1985, Lillian Vernon opened a retail store in New Rochelle, New York, to take care of excess inventory. Katz expects the store to reach $500,000 in annual sales by 1988 and is preparing for the day when America will become saturated with mail-order catalogs.

By the early 1990s, she hopes to have stores nationally. In the summer of 1987, Lillian Vernon, Inc. went public and simultaneously announced plans for a new distribution center in Virginia Beach, Virginia. Lillian describes the facility as being 454,000 square feet on a 52-acre site. When the company went public (with shares trading on the American Stock Exchange), Lillian and her two sons divested themselves of 30 percent of the ownership of the business. Their 70 percent stock ownership, however, still gives the family effective control. Entrepreneur Lillian Vernon Katz remains chief executive officer of the company she started thirty-seven years ago with a $495 investment in a mail-order advertisement of a belt and a handbag.

4

FAITH POPCORN

She Discerns the Future

Faith Popcorn

Faith Popcorn tunes in on emerging consumer trends. Brain-Reserve, the company she founded, does a unique job of market research by determining with remarkable accuracy not only what the consumer wants now—but will want in the future. Her clients include manufacturers of some of the best-known consumer products in the world such as Campbell Soup, Kellogg's Colgate-Palmolive, General Foods, The Nestlé Company, Polaroid, Seagram's, Timex, and Water Pik.

The uniqueness of BrainReserve lies in the methodology of the organization where Popcorn has assembled a staff of talented research associates and an adjunct group of several hundred consumers with whom the company conducts 2,000 individual interviews each year, and whose input not only provides the basis for solving clients' problems but has assisted in formulating some of the remarkably accurate forecasts she has made since 1980. For example, Faith predicted:

- a big market for salt-free products
- the return of flashy cars
- the popularity of older TV stars in a national de-emphasis on youth
- media rooms for the home
- "nouvelle cuisine"
- padded shoulders in women's clothes
- preventive medicine
- the decline of white wine and the return of glamourous mixed drinks
- the failure of New Coke (it turned out to be the fiasco of the decade)
- health-oriented, take-out, fast food

Looking even further ahead, Popcorn has predicted a developing market for a car that is specially positioned for women—the safest in the world—with airbags, an SOS device, and built-in baby seats. "By the year 2000, the bathroom will be regarded as an antistress or leisure center," says this visionary woman whom *The New Yorker* suggests has been irresistibly shaping our lives.[1] Popcorn loves to predict trends in foods and points out that yogurt's nutritional value, for instance, has not been fully exploited. "Yogurt-based products such as sauces and dressings are not here yet; but yogurt is a good low-fat base for a lot of foods like veggie-dip and potato toppings." Popcorn even predicts that a Frank Perdue of *fish* will emerge in the years ahead!

Faith Popcorn appears to fit one typical characteristic of the entrepreneur—bright and determined, she had an idea she believed was marketable. Convinced that the advertising agencies where she had been working for a few years were really not sufficiently in touch with consumers properly to advise clients about effective marketing strategies, Popcorn saw the advantages of helping clients' businesses by thoroughly understanding consumer trends and how those trends will determine future product successes. She finds distasteful the tendencies of some advertising agencies not to get close enough to the *consumer*. As she expresses this view, "When I was in the ad-agency business, I saw the terrible errors clients made in accepting manipulative advice of the agency people, and I became convinced there was a niche for a service that would provide an honest resource that comes only from the consumer, reporting directly how the consumer responds to different ideas." Her dissatisfaction with her agency job, coupled with a desire to control her own destiny in which she had profound confidence, inspired her, and with a limited amount of starting capital from her own savings, she began BrainReserve in 1975. There was then no *futurist* in the business, no one who applied the future to new products currently being marketed, and BrainReserve was ready to fill this need. Constantly dedicated to its mission of thoroughly understanding consumer trends, BrainReserve has grown and flourished under Faith Popcorn's direction to become number fifty-four in the *Savvy* annual list of the sixty top U. S. businesses run by women.[2]

Popcorn, a name one can hardly forget, is one of Faith's cherished assets. Her family name was originally "Cornea, and when her Italian immigrant grandfather passed through Ellis Island and was asked to give his name, he responded to the immigration officer with a blank stare, not understanding a word of English. "What do they call you in Italy?" an interpreter shouted in Italian. "Papa Cornea," he replied. Thus, Faith grew up as the daughter of the Papacornea family. In her late teens, her roommate began calling her "Popcorn" and the name stuck. Today, she admits that this astonishing name attracts attention and only helps her business.

A major function of BrainReserve is the repositioning of consumer products. Popcorn discovered that the history of marketing is filled with "prehistoric beasts"—products that disappeared long ago because of improper analysis of consumer-demand trends. As she relates it: "Take Bab-O, for instance, the biggest powder cleanser product of its time. Had the makers foreseen that American housewives were ready for *easier* cleaning, Bab-O might have survived. After all, it was the 1950s—the era of burgeoning technology like Sputnik, stereophonic sound, kitchen clothes washers and dryers, dishwashers and television, and stains without strains. So it was not surprising that, by the mid-fifties Comet and Ajax, the easy cleaners, eclipsed Bab-O whose marketers failed to reposition the product."

Among winners in the repositioning race of that era (as cited by Popcorn) were, for instance, Marlboro which propelled itself from a red filter tip that was specially targeted to women, and then with a minor market share, to the leader of the industry, by focusing on the Marlboro *man*—and a correct assumption that men need the reassurance that smoking *filter* cigarettes is *masculine*, even individualistic. Another example, cites Popcorn, was Clairol with the memorable campaign featuring the headline: "Does She or Doesn't She?" "Previously, the only women who dyed their hair had been either blue-haired or those of questionable reputation. Clairol's repositioning of hair coloring made it a legitimate option for self-respecting, proper American women of any age."

Popcorn maintains that marketers should look carefully at a product or brand for indications of decline. "By the time sales of it decline, it may be too late. How do you know when it's time to restage? That's where BrainReserve comes in and provides an honest evaluation of a client's product and comes up with answers as to how the product really fits *today's* market-place, and how it will probably fare in the months and years ahead.

The core of BrainReserve's remarkable success lies in its unique methodology which relies on hundreds of real, live consumers throughout America with whom BrainReserve's researchers consult on a continuing basis, and who provide the company with ideas, attitudes, and recommendations that are of great importance in the decision-making processes of clients. In consequence, BrainReserve has the advantage of knowing why consumers like a product, how they use it, and what does or doesn't appeal to them. Popcorn likes to cite as an example Gordon McGovern, chief executive officer of Campbell Soup, who personally and regularly shops in supermarkets all across the country. "He knows firsthand what consumers want. Also, he's the kind who insists that all of his executives in all departments do likewise. Too few top executives realize how important this is."

Faith Popcorn was born in New York of parents who were both lawyers. Her father, whom Faith describes as her first role model, left his practice as a criminal lawyer to work for a U. S. Government intelligence agency in China. While still a toddler, Faith and her mother joined her father there and she was later placed in the Convent of the Sacred Heart in Shanghai. Returning to New York at the age of six, she entered the public school system. Her secondary school years were spent at the High School of Performing Arts where she confesses she was always in trouble. "I was the kid in the back of the classroom who was always talking to other kids and the teacher would hear only me and select me as the culprit for punishment." Her extracurricular activities at the High School of Performing Arts consisted mainly of writing plays, going to plays, and being dramatic. "I wanted to be an actress in those days—because I'm sort of a ham and enjoy attention," she confesses. "My boyfriends were the 'weirdo' types, and I may have been influenced here by my father, who as a criminal lawyer loved both trouble and representing 'oddballs' who got into trouble. I was very close to him and was crushed emotionally when his life was tragically terminated in an automobile accident when I was eighteen. I did manage to finish college with a major in English and worked part time in my grandfather's haberdashery on New York's Lower East side. This experience convinced me that I would only be happy in business—my own business."

Popcorn's first job out of college was with Grey Advertising, where she learned how to write advertising copy, supervise people, and how to make full use of public relations opportunities. She mentions one former colleague, a man with whom she still retains a relationship, who she claims "taught me to keep out of trouble." Popcorn admits to having once been married but only for a short time and long ago.

On the subject of intuitive decision making (to which a subsequent chapter of this book is devoted), Faith Popcorn confesses she used to work *solely* on intuition and that it has only been through the process of the research aspects of her business that she has come, by necessity, to temper intuition with logical analysis. "Balancing intuition with logical analysis plus hard work, lots of determination, and self-confidence seems to be the key to our success," says founder Popcorn. "Another factor is that I have given my business the highest priority of time during my waking hours—superseding my personal life, my family, friends, and all leisure activities."

NOTES

1. "Talk of the Town," *The New Yorker*, July 7, 1986, p. 22.
2. Kelly B. Walker, "America's Top Women Business Owners," *Savvy*, April 1986, p. 39.

5

GERALDINE STUTZ

She Bought the Store

Geraldine Stutz

In 1957 Maxey Jarman, then the chief executive officer of the Genesco conglomerate, spotted Geraldine (Jerry) Stutz as a very special and talented young thirty-three-year-old executive when she was divisional president of a chain of I. Miller stores. Genesco had been on a binge of buying up retail stores and suffered a real headache with Henri Bendel, an ancient, "carriage-trade" store of fashion located in two aging 57th Street buildings just west of fashionable Fifth Avenue in New York which Genesco had acquired in the early 1950s.

Jarman believed that businesses catering to women would be better run by women and picked Stutz for the job of converting Bendel's $1.5 million loss on sales of $3 million per year into a viable situation. "It was everybody's favorite store," says Stutz whimsically, "but nobody had been in it for twenty years." Although she had been a fashion model, a fashion-magazine editor, and a shoe-chain manager, she had never had the merchandising training that is characteristic of fashion-store top executives. But she had something else—the incredible intuitive talent of a great visionary. Looking over a heap of high-priced matronly dresses and other apparel, she conjured up a vision of what the store ought to be, and with Jarman's full confidence and bankrolling transformed the main floor of Bendel's into her famous "Street of Shops" (the skeptical competitors first dubbed it the "Street of Flops"), an eye-catching labyrinth of individual boutiques containing trendy and chic merchandise for style-conscious women, like Stutz herself. "I knew instinctively that we must be the kind of store that I myself would like to shop in and that it must be a cozy, intimate place with friendly, personal service to cater to sophisticated, small-sized women who love clothes," says Stutz. She believes that the core of her success in bringing Bendel's to profitability—a process that took five years—was in "choosing terrific talent and providing an environment for them to do their best work. When I couldn't afford to have the best, I hired young talent who I knew were going to be the best."

By the time Stutz had brought Bendel's into the black, Genesco, like many other conglomerates of the mid–1970s, was in deep financial trouble, having acquired more businesses than it had the expertise to manage profitably. A tight cash position required Genesco to sell off its retail operations, including Bonwit Teller, Plymouth Shops, and Henri Bendel's. At this point, Barney's, the famous men's apparel store on 17th Street, was looking for expansion into the women's field and made an offer to Genesco for Bendel's. Jerry Stutz, with the help of a group of Swiss investors and every cent she had at the time, matched Barney's offer, and in July 1980 bought the store she had managed for twenty-three years.

Ever since she was a child, Stutz has been an overachiever. "My mother was always ambitious for me," she recalls. "Mom, herself a middle-management executive of the DuPont Company with twelve people reporting to her, had always pushed me, unlike my father—who was the passive type." Her mother encouraged her to be competitive in every activity and to take chances; Stutz gives credit for her early drive to what she likes to call "Mother Superior," her own mother, and "Mother Church," the Roman Catholic education training and its characteristic discipline. "At an early age, I didn't dream of anything but being a performer and doing what was expected of me. I was always in the top 5 percent of my class, editor of the school newspaper, president of my class, and captain of the swimming team. Mundelein College—run by the Sisters of Charity and an all-women's school—awarded me a scholarship, and though I was marvelously good in the liberal arts, I had no flair for math and science. They were my great weaknesses, but I never apologized for them because my gifts have been abundant."

Stutz adds that her real education came after college when she went to work for the publishing firm of Condé Nast—an organization she describes as "the perfect pattern of a convent school." Here were recruited bright young women, instructed and led by "Mother Superior" types. "All of us were given a complete fashion education—in exchange for which we gave loyalty and obedience. Although the pay was dismal, it was a first-class life that sent us all over the world and taught us a style of life that I brought to Bendel's."

After purchasing Bendel's from Genesco in 1980, Stutz found her spot a lonely one. Her financial partners in Switzerland knew little about retailing and she had to take on the added burden of financial responsibility, an area where she admits that she really didn't know what she was doing. "So I learned—because of necessity, I simply had to," she says. "Sure we had crises—lots of them—but in retailing you teach yourself to know that the day is not important—only the basic objectives of the enterprise. And when business is bad, you 'soldier on.' Also, you don't go overboard emotionally when times are good. Overall, our business during the past five years was terrific, except for 1984 which was terrible from the viewpoint of profitability."

Stutz's keen intuition and foresight told her in 1985 that the one-store fashion retailer could not survive in the same arena against the buying power of such stores as Bergdorf-Goodman, Bloomingdale's, Saks Fifth Avenue, and Neiman-Marcus. Not having sufficient capital to expand Bendel's into a national chain, she accepted a purchase offer in the summer of 1985 from The Limited which had the financial strength to expand Bendel's into every fashion capital of the world. Stutz came up a liquid multimillionairess—the announced price for the acquisition of Bendel's by The Limited was $2.4 million in cash, plus a 3-year $800,000 promissory note, with a five-year contract to run Bendel's and preside over its expansion under the direction of The Limited whose other properties include Lerner Stores, Lane Bryant, and Victoria's Secret.

Geraldine Stutz has never lost her entrepreneurial spirit, and at age sixty-five exudes a disarming aura of determination and reserved self-confidence. Her personal life is shared with a large circle of friends and she is a gracious hostess at her East Side townhouse, and on weekends at her country place in Roxbury, Connecticut. She rides to work in taxis, having abandoned a car and driver because knowing they were waiting for her made her feel guilty. Her outside interests include board memberships on the National Council for the Arts and the Costume Institute of the Metropolitan Museum of Art in New York. A twelve-year marriage to David Gibbs ended in 1977. Commenting on it, Stutz says, "I wouldn't have missed it for anything and there were lots of terrific things about it, but it simply did not endure." For a woman as busy as she is, Stutz manages to spend a lot of time with books and will read four or five books at one time, skipping from one to the other. She claims this inspiration comes from "one of those wonderful nuns who told her, as a child, to read, read, and keep on reading."

Those same nuns, along with her mother and the "Mothers Superior" of Condé Nast Publications, more than any other factors moulded the character of Geraldine Stutz, the overachiever who came to New York in the early 1950s with a few dollars in her handbag but never, for one moment, believed that she would not continue to be in the top 5 percent of her class!

POSTSCRIPT

Entrepreneurs who build successful businesses that are later acquired by giant corporations seldom fit into the characteristic, bureaucratic structure of billion dollar corporations like The Limited, whose founder and chief executive, Leslie Wexner, comes from an entirely different mold than Geraldine Stutz. Shortly after my interview with Stutz for this book in April 1986, it became obvious that the inevitable was happening. According to *New York Magazine*, "the first clue came around the time of Limited's acquisition of Bendel's. Stutz and Wexner appeared at the same party at Maxim's and everyone greeted Stutz, but few people seemed to recognize her vastly wealthier and more successful employer."[1]

As tension grew out of the many imposed changes at Bendel's under Wexner's direction, Stutz could see that oil and water did not mix well and requested that The Limited buy out her contract, which had four more years to go. It was further reported by *New York Magazine* that "the day she left the store, to avoid making a fuss, she went down the back stairs, walked out the employee's entrance, and got into a cab. With her departure, that special fashion snobbery she had so successfully built into Bendel's went with her.[2]

Shortly afterward, Stutz was named president and publisher of a new division of Random House, Panache Press. Here, she has the opportunity of employing her great entrepreneurial talents to develop books on such subjects as fashion, decor, entertaining, the arts, and social history.

NOTES

1. Jesse Kornbluth, "The Battle of Bendel's," *New York Magazine*, February 23, 1987, p. 29.

2. Ibid., p. 31.

6

DEBRAH LEE CHARATAN

She Made Millions before Age Thirty

Debrah Lee Charatan

Debrah Charatan is a unique individual as well as a unique entrepreneur, but most of all, she is a unique success. Operating in what had been characteristically a male-dominated industry, in 1980 she founded Bach Realty, Inc., a real estate brokerage firm which, according to the August 1986 issue of *INC. Magazine*, grossed over $200 million annually. Yet Debrah is now thirty-one years old.

Her firm has some forty employees—predominantly women—all of whom make 250 calls a day contacting commercial real estate buyers and sellers. Active as she is in her business, she still finds time to serve on the boards of four major charitable organizations, make numerous television and radio appearances, respond to a constant stream of requests for professional speaking engagements, serve as an adjunct faculty member of Queens College, and keep track of her four-year-old son with whom she still spends several hours every day.

Debrah Charatan has known little but hard work since she was a child. The youngest of three, she was born in Brooklyn in 1957 of Polish immigrant parents who had fled the ravages of the Holocaust in the previous decade. While still attending high school, she started her practice of working eighty hours a week, not only for financial reasons, but because, as she confesses, she "loved" working then, as she does now. Her favorite job was tutoring other kids for $4 an hour. That was easy and relaxing. The tougher job was on weekends when she had to get out of bed at 4 A.M. in order to present herself at a Queens bakery that opened for business at 5 A.M. Since she worked full time from high school on, her college education took seven years of night classes. She graduated in 1980 from Baruch College with honors.

Debrah Charatan exhibits many of the characteristics common to the successful entrepreneur. She has always enjoyed independence and autonomy, and very much enjoys the freedom of being her own boss. While she takes chances, she denies that she is a gambler, and points out that all the risks she has ever taken have been "educated risks," that is, very well researched. In presiding over Bach Realty, she is perceived by most as being tough but fair. Above all, she tries never to avoid issues, but rather to confront them squarely as they arise. In fact, she seems to enjoy the exhilaration of the challenge in problem solving. "Whenever problems arise," says Charatan, "I don't let them sit and fester, but strive to get them behind me as soon as possible, so that I can be free to get back into the stream of opportunities that comes our way."

Debrah Charatan believes strongly that work itself is the best education. Referring to her own achievement of earning a bachelor's degree by attending college at night over a seven-year period: "My major regret was that I didn't take even more business courses. I find that everything I learned helps me immeasurably in my business."

Charatan entered the world of real estate as a secretary in a real estate agency, but soon advanced to managing buildings under contract to her employer when the latter realized that Debrah had capabilities far beyond those of a secretary. (Part of the function of commercial real estate agencies is to act not only as brokers in the sale or lease of commercial property, but to provide management and maintenance of buildings for clients.) She is grateful to those who helped her.

I have been fortunate that my life has been filled with excellent mentors. One of the many who taught me about real estate was my friend Pat Fields. When Pat was with the firm, I had been her protegé. When she left the firm, I was left on my own. Having a lot of self-confidence, it turned out to be a blessing in disguise because it propelled me into starting my own real estate firm. A business acquaintance loaned me $2,000 to begin in a tiny basement office on Madison Avenue. All I had was a typewriter, a telephone, a makeshift desk, and a determined mission to become the best commercial real estate broker that I could be. I began calling building owners all over the New York City area to see if they would sell, then called other people to see if they would buy.

Two years later, Bach Realty had a whole floor in the same Madison Avenue building, a sales staff of twenty-two women, and Bach Realty was well on its way to becoming the number one commercial realty firm in New York.

Her personal life is hectic and complex, but yet paradoxically simple and uncomplicated. Although she takes no vacations, she rents a house for the summer in Southampton, New York, with her son.

Above all, Debrah Charatan is a devoted person. She is devoted to her clients, her employees, her friends, her family, and most of all, to her son. Her devotion is intensely reciprocated by those who are fortunate enough to be involved with her. In the final analysis, it could well be that this fierce devotion makes her the unique success she is.

Charatan places much faith in the intuitive aspects of decision making. "I must have a *feeling* about things—without a frame of reference to facts that are on the surface—and here I think women are much better at it than men," she says. Asked to explain this conviction, she responded with a cryptic "women are *nurturers* and *creators*, and take the *human* factor more seriously than men."

7

JOSIE NATORI

She Made a Blouse into a Nightshirt

Josie Natori

Josie Alemenda Cruz Natori was born in Manila, the Philippines, in 1947 into a family where the concept of the working woman was an accustomed way of life. Her mother came from a family of affluence and prestige, and her father was a building contractor who was completely and successfully self-made.

At the age of nine, Josie was known as a child prodigy, an accomplished pianist, who performed concertos with the Manila Symphony Orchestra. All through school she was on the scholastic honors list, always a leader and officer in school organizations, and always dedicated to the idea of someday having her own business. "My grandmother was my real mentor, however," says Natori. "Grandma was a truly liberated woman and matriarch who said that a woman should never ask her husband for anything and should earn things herself through making her own money."

At the age of seventeen, she arrived in New York to study at Manhattanville College, then an all-women's college in Purchase, New York, where Josie majored in economics, hoping some day to have her own brokerage business. She graduated in 1968 and went immediately to a $6,500 job with Bache Securities in New York where her performance was so impressive that her employer sent her to Manila six months later to open a branch for the company. At the tender age of twenty-one, she was already the branch's only broker.

Returning to New York in 1971, she left Bache to join Merrill Lynch, and by 1976 was a vice-president earning in excess of $100,000 a year. She had also married Kenneth Natori, whom she had met during her Wall Street days, and had borne a son. By 1977 Josie Natori could see that her dreams of starting her own business were not likely to be in Wall Street, so she chose the hectic, competitive atmosphere of New York's garment industry where she had no experience, training, or contacts. In choosing her entrepreneurial path, she had two criteria: the business would have to contribute something to her homeland and it would have to have something special and unique to rise above competition. The Philippines is famous for its intricate stitchery and embroidery, so Natori began to look for some way to transform that craftsmanship into fashions that would appeal to American women.

Through family contacts in Manila, she had a number of embroidered blouses sent to her in New York. When she showed her samples to a Bloomingdale's buyer, she was told that they were too short in length for the American woman's figure. "Make them longer—even as long as nightshirts," said the buyer. With a flash of intuition inspired by this remark, Josie went into the high-fashion lingerie and sleepwear business. Her first showroom was her Manhattan apartment's living room where she took orders from Neiman-Marcus, Lord & Taylor, and Saks Fifth Avenue. Other orders followed from West Coast buyers and from fashion stores in Canada. Saks was so excited over Josie's collection that it took a full-page advertisement in the *New York Times* announcing her opening presentation in all their thirty-four stores. It was about this time that the factory in Manila was started.

With funds she had earned in Wall Street, coupled with a "loan" from her husband who was by this time a senior executive with Shearson-Lehman Company, Josie invested $150,000 to start The Natori Company. In March of 1978, she leased a small showroom and six years later, with sales and profits zooming, she moved into new offices that reflect the posh, high-quality, and chic aspects of The Natori Company's merchandise and that of its chic founder and president. The company faced a disaster during 1983 when production in the Manila factory which employs 600 workers was paralyzed for two months following the assassination of Benigno Aquino, husband of the current president, Corazon Aquino. This event triggered political disturbances and demonstrations against the former president Marcos. Many factories came to a halt. Natori did not give up but struggled on, and more recently, under the new political regime, with Natori's factory committed to excellence, the prized Golden Shell Award has been made in each of the past two years to The Natori Company. This award is given annually by the Philippine government to companies that excel in their individual industries.

Josie Natori explains her success in terms of her early training. "I was born a *doer*, not a follower, and I had a high need for achievement. I think I loved challenges more than money—which explains why I left Wall Street to enter the apparel industry, with no background in the latter. Thank God, I took accounting and other business courses in college—I could never have survived without them."

Josie Natori claims that in decision making she tends to rely on intuition and "gut" feelings as much as cognition and analysis. She admits to having made lots of mistakes but, she says, "I learn from them and feel more secure later when I move on to the next step. One thing I found difficult to get used to in apparel is the inconsistencies of the industry. One day we can have so many orders from stores, we agonize over how we can fill them all. Another day we have just the opposite, but I'm able to overcome. Here is where my husband has been a tower of strength." In 1985 Kenneth Natori left a high-paying executive job in Wall Street to join The Natori Company as its chief financial officer. "Even though I'm an independent person, I lean on Ken for moral support, encouragement, and advice. He recognizes my strengths and I recognize his; most importantly, I can honestly say that our marriage was made in heaven!"

Josie Natori at age forty—ninety-eight pounds of energy—wants the continuous challenge of expanding her business. Already The Natori Company has extended its product line into slippers, less expensive multipurpose sleepwear and loungewear for the contemporary customer, travel bags, and linens; and more recently into a line of body and bath products, plus a fragrance simply called "Natori." One can even find a Natori boutique in Bloomingdale's New York store, and according to *Savvy* magazine, Josie's eight-year-old company has achieved sales revenues of about $12 million a year.[1]

NOTE

1. "Strange Bedfellows," *Savvy*, February 1986.

8

DIANE VON FURSTENBERG

She Relies on Intuition

Diane Von Furstenberg

Diane Von Furstenberg is a woman who admits to being full of contradictions. "I don't like greed, but I'm greedy," she told me. "I'm still growing at age forty and I'm ambitious, but I must find a new way to reconcile my work with the woman I am, and I'm now trying to find my way."

In the mid-seventies, Princess Diane Von Furstenberg was selling 25,000 of her little wrap dresses a week, but her most famous creation was herself, as she exploited the title she acquired by marrying Prince Egon Von Furstenberg (whom she divorced in 1983 after a ten-year separation).

Still a multimillionairess, she has made and lost millions, and has done it mainly on her own. Detesting the problems that are part of heading up a manufacturing company, Diane now licenses her name and provides the design talent for her licensees which include manufacturers of dresses, sportswear, lingerie, cosmetics, luggage, costume jewelry, watches, hosiery, handbags, eyeglasses, and home furnishings. The annual sales estimates of products bearing the Von Furstenberg label range from $250 million to $300 million. She also operates a small couture boutique located on New York's Fifth Avenue near her design studio.

The mother of two teenagers to whom she is completely devoted, Diane lives the affluent life in a large Manhattan Fifth Avenue apartment and on a fifty-three acre estate in New Milford, Connecticut. She travels abroad several times a year to derive design inspiration and ideas for her licensees. "I dislike the whole idea of being a manager," admits Von Furstenberg. "I think I know what women want and I've got a very good sense of design and can create what they want. That's why all I have now in the way of a business organization is my design studio, so I'm really nothing but a glorified consultant."

When Brussels-born Diane Halfin Von Furstenberg speaks of her early childhood, she believes that even her birth was somewhat of a miracle. "My mother spent fourteen months in a German concentration camp and when she was released at the age of nineteen, she weighed forty-four pounds. I was born two years later although she wasn't supposed to have a child so soon." Diane Halfin found her childhood boring. "I was in a hurry to grow up. My overly strict mother forbade me to go out with boys or even wear makeup—but she did force me to be self-reliant. Independence and freedom were very important to my mother after her terrible ordeal at Auschwitz—and she had great faith in my future. I remember her saying, when I was eleven years old: 'You will always get what you want.' "

When her parents were divorced, Diane was fifteen and was dispatched by her father—a Belgian commodities broker—to boarding schools in England, Spain, and Switzerland. At age twenty, she went to work briefly for the American financier Bernie Cornfeld who had built a fortune for himself in Investors Overseas Services, a mutual fund management company that sponsored the internationally successful Fund of Funds in the 1960s. While in Geneva, Diane attended the university where she met Prince Egon Von Furstenberg whose Prussian title dates to the twelfth century, and whose fortune—far less ancient—stems from his mother, Clara Agnelli Nuvoletti, of the Fiat Motor Company fortune. On July 15, 1969, Diane Halfin, already pregnant, became Princess Diane Von Furstenberg in a fashionable Geneva wedding. "I felt low and miserable," recalls Diane bitterly. "People were saying that Egon was young, attractive, rich, and from an aristocratic family. How could he marry this Jewish girl who came from nothing?"

The hurt to her psyche channeled the twenty-two-year-old bride into action. Immediately, she went to work as an apprentice for Angelo Ferretti, a prominent Italian textile manufacturer near Lake Como, where she gained considerable knowledge about the printing of fabrics. She and Egon moved to New York in 1970 and brought with them several silk-jersey dresses made from Ferretti's fabric. Working through a contact, she showed them to Diana Vreeland, then the editor of *Vogue*, who advised her to open a little showroom in a New York hotel and contact a few store buyers. *Vogue* ran an editorial on one of her items—the little wrap dress—and the career of Diane Von Furstenberg was launched.

The beginnings of her first enterprise were modest indeed,

and she operated on a strictly hand-to-mouth basis. Her dresses were designed over her dining room table in her New York apartment and made in Italy. Diane would wait at the customs shed at JFK Airport for them to arrive and be reshipped to her American customers. With a $10,000 pawn-shop loan on one of her diamond rings, plus a gift from her father in Belgium, Diane set up on Seventh Avenue. Her business quickly expanded. Meanwhile, the Von Furstenbergs became the darlings of New York's café society. Although they soon separated, Diane capitalized on her position as a "princess," and merchandised her title while becoming her own public-relations director. She hit the cover of *Newsweek* in March of 1976, thus becoming a national celebrity. By this time, her sales had topped $65 million and stores throughout the country were stocking up on Diane Von Furstenberg dresses. Then disaster struck. The year 1977, in which the apparel industry suffered from a depressed national economy, coupled with bad planning on her part, found her stuck with a $4 million inventory. "I panicked," she admits now. "It was pretty bad, but I was sure I could somehow overcome it. But, I was really a child in distress."

She did survive the blow and, with the help of her new boyfriend, reorganized her company. Relying on the strength of the Von Furstenberg name, she negotiated a contract with Sears, Roebuck & Co. to develop a home-accessories line and sold all but her cosmetics and fragrance businesses to licensees. One of these, Puritan Fashions, a major dress manufacturing concern, guaranteed her royalties of $1 million a year to manufacture dresses under her name, and by 1980 Diane Von Furstenberg's signature products were grossing nearly $250 million a year. Meanwhile, her cosmetics company, while selling about $20 million of Von Furstenberg products, was sold "for a lot of money" to a manufacturer to whom she licensed her name.

Reflecting on the transformation from her somewhat turbulent success as an entrepreneur to that of a consultant, Von Furstenberg admits to a deficient knowledge of finance and accounting. She claims to do everything "on intuition" and the author Roy Rowan, commenting on her sudden acclaim and consequent tailspin in the late 1970s, suggests she has an impeccable sense of timing as a style-setter who chose to "run rather than cope" when she got out of manufacturing in favor of licensing.[1] When I questioned her about Rowan's comments, Diane said that she firmly shares the conviction that intuition, more than cognition, has always governed her decision making. Writing about herself in her own *Cosmopolitan* article, she stated: "My best quality is also my worst—crazy impulsiveness; I'm an emotional investor—I'm not a saver. I take risks; I dive; I'm passionate—yet it's an act of passion that makes things happen."[2]

Diane Von Furstenberg still wants to make things happen, but she's unsure of her direction, and appears to be a complete fatalist. "Life is like a river," she says, "on which we sometimes hurl downstream like a leaf, fragile and unprotected."

NOTES

1. Roy Rowan, *The Intuitive Manager* (Boston: Little, Brown & Co., 1986), p. 135.

2. *Cosmopolitan*, November 1985, p. 399.

9

MURIEL SIEBERT

Rebel of Wall Street

Muriel Siebert

Muriel Siebert broke the sex barrier to become the first woman member of the New York Stock Exchange. She has made all the money she needs, operates her own discount brokerage business, has three honorary doctorates, but she never finished college. Born the younger of two daughters and raised in Cleveland, Ohio, during the years of the Great Depression, her father practiced dentistry and also had a degree in engineering.

She was Cleveland's yo-yo champion at the age of ten, played the clarinet, and starred on the school tennis team.[1] "My grades in school were always A's if I was interested—otherwise, I would only scrape through. But I was always good at numbers which still seem to leap off the page at me, and when I attended Western Reserve University, I focused on accounting and economics courses. This was during the war years when my father—because he was also an engineer—worked four hours each day in a defense plant in addition to his dental practice. He died suddenly and without any estate, and I had to drop out of college to help support my mother who had become ill."

Siebert's first full-time job was that of an accountant in a small Cleveland company. "I fought a lot of battles because they paid men more than women for doing the same work. I switched jobs a few times and, in the process, developed a kind of independence which in 1954 brought me to New York in my old Studebaker with $500 in my purse." Siebert's first job was with Bache and Company, who hired her as a research analyst at $65 a week. Six years later, she became the first woman partner of Stearns and Company (now Bear-Stearns). In 1962 she became a partner of Finkle and Company. "I learned about trading stocks at the trading table from Davy Finkle. The trading table is where everyone should go to learn this business," advises Siebert. Women partners on Wall Street were a rare phenomenon—just the kind of challenge that would spark Siebert's strong determination. Over the course of the next few years, she built up a substantial commission business. In 1967 Gerald Tsai, the famous financier and founder of the Manhattan Fund, now chairman and chief executive officer of Primerica, Inc., gave her the idea of having her own business. " 'Mickie, why make all that money for others when you can have it all for yourself,' Jerry asked me." So, with $445,000, much of it borrowed, and with considerable resistance from some segments of the all-male membership of the New York Stock Exchange, Muriel Siebert bought a seat and became its first woman member. "I was delightfully outnumbered," she says, "1,365 men and me." Subsequently, she formed her own firm, Muriel Siebert and Company.

Siebert insists she never had a business plan or strategy. "There was no strategy," she says. "I stumbled along—saw this and grabbed it, saw that and grabbed it—but I was never afraid to take risks, or admit to having made a mistake, or take on a new challenge." In 1975 commissions for trading of securities became under New York State law a negotiable transaction between brokers and clients. Here was a window through which she saw new opportunities. She immediately announced she would buy or sell securities in larger blocks at commissions far below that of other prominent brokerage houses. She launched an ad campaign featuring pictures of herself cutting a hundred dollar bill in half—much to the chagrin of most of her colleagues in the stock exchange.

In March of 1977, New York's Democratic governor Hugh Carey asked Mickie, who is a Republican, to take over the job of superintendent of New York's banks. As a state government official, she was required to divest the stock she owned and put her own company into a blind trust in order to comply with conflict of interest regulations. Her new office's jurisdiction included more than 103 savings banks, 104 commercial banks, and the New York branches of 139 foreign banks. She also took an enormous salary cut to $50,000 a year. "This move cost me a lot of money," she recounts, "but by that time, I had enough money and a strong sense of community responsibility and wanted a new challenge."

Siebert stayed on this job for five years, and as Morris D. Crawford, former chairman of the Bowery Savings Bank, told me, "Mickie was the best bank superintendent New York State ever had. During her regime, not one bank failed, and she handled with great ingenuity and tenacity the many rescue mergers that saved troubled banks from going under during those difficult years."

In 1982 Siebert resigned her job to run in a Republican primary for the U.S. Senate, coming in second in a three-way race. When asked if she would still like to be a senator, she replied:

I may tackle it again. A senator can make a difference in the conduct of our country. Trouble is, many of them only care about getting re-elected. I view this as a total disgrace. The great problems America faces, like the fiscal and trade deficits, are not being addressed by our politicians because they lack the guts to do the right thing for this and future generations. The only way you can get quality in office is to elevate pay schedules—otherwise you get people with money or those who can't succeed in other fields and have to work their way through the system.

Siebert likes to repeat this message in her numerous speaking engagements before young people at colleges and universities. "I insist we should work hard to preserve the system and try to make it better. Show me a better one if you can—it enabled me to come here with $500 bucks and without a college degree and yet make a lot of money. I tell students to get out there and get active!"

Muriel Siebert organizes her busy life as the head of her brokerage firm to permit her to be active in a host of community activities. These include the Boy Scouts of America, the Committee of 200 (an elite group of successful women executives), Manhattan College (trustee & chairperson of the Finance Committee), Financial Accounting Standards Board, New York University Board of Overseers, Metropolitan Museum of Art (Business Committee), New York State Business Council, Small Business Forum of the New York Board of Trade, and many others. She has been awarded honorary doctorates by St. John's University, Molloy College, and St. Bonaventure University.

She has little time for recreation, but owns a weekend home in East Hampton, New York. Questioned about personal matters, such as love and marriage, Mickie admits to having "come close" a couple of times. "When I was about thirty-eight, I was going with a guy who wanted to settle down and raise a family.

I realized that if I wanted a family I better get married *now*. But I quickly decided that if I was going to get married *just to have children*, I wasn't going to get married." She has a pilot's license, but because of her many other activities, she gave it up after she learned to solo.

Gary Brody, senior vice-president at the Bowery Savings Bank in New York, who worked for Siebert in the state banking department says: "Being oppressed as the first woman member of the stock exchange tempered and honed her as much as anything. When it comes to business decisions, she's very tough and businesslike—an exterior that hides a person who's very giving, very generous."[2] Siebert recently donated $5,000 to the National Museum of Women in the Arts, Washington, D.C., after a three-minute telephone request. When asked about it, she said, "I believe in it. What am I going to do with my money—take it with me?"

NOTES

1. *Look Magazine* published her picture with a yo-yo in the late 1970s which became a source of kidding by the male members of the stock exchange. Now, whenever anyone mentions yo-yo, she hands them a yo-yo with her picture on it.

2. *Working Woman*, April 1986, p. 64.

10

MARY KAY ASH

You Can Do It!

Mary Kay Ash

Mary Kay Ash is an extraordinary shining star in the world's cosmetic industry. Mary Kay Cosmetics, the company she formed in 1963, registers over $300 million in annual sales and provides an income from its marketing program to some 200,000 women throughout the United States, Canada, the United Kingdom, West Germany, and Argentina. Mary Kay herself, believed to be now in her seventies (she refuses to admit her true age), lives by the Golden Rule, loves her job so much she claims she would do it for no salary, and preaches a theme that the seeds of greatness are planted in every human being and that "a woman can do anything she makes up her mind to do."[1]

As a child, Mary Kay lived in Houston, where it was necessary for her mother, Lila Wagner, to work fourteen hours a day in the restaurant she owned in order to support herself, her four children, and an invalid husband—Mary Kay's father—who had to live for three years in a sanatorium for tuberculosis patients. "I was seven years old then, but I took care of my father while Mother was at the restaurant. My only contact with her was by phone. I can still her hear telling me to get out the big pot, use two potatoes, two onions, and take a cup of cream off the top of the milk," she recalls. "She always told me in great detail how to do things I needed to do and would end every conversation with the words 'You can do it, honey.' That has become the guiding theme of my life."

As a teenager, Mary Kay Wagner was obviously a superachiever. "I was a member of the debating team and drill team. I sold tickets for all the athletic games and I always sold the most. I had to have straight A's in my grades and would often stay up until 3:00 A.M. to make sure my papers were perfect." she relates. When she finished high school, all her friends were going off to college. "I couldn't because of a lack of finances, even though I wanted to be a doctor and do something great. At eighteen, I married a local radio star—Ben Rogers, the 'Elvis Presley' of Houston in those days. I thought he was a great catch, but later found out that the only thing he was interested in was guitar strings." The marriage lasted through eleven years and three children, and after Ben returned from military service in World War II, he wanted a divorce—so there was Mary Kay, on her own with three children and few marketable skills. She had tried taking some premed courses at the University of Houston while Ben was in the service, but the dean persuaded her not to strive for a career in medicine. "I couldn't stand cutting up those frogs, didn't like lab work, so it probably was a good decision." A friend told her about Stanley Home Products, which involved conducting demonstrations in people's homes, so she tried this while taking a job as secretary to the pastor of the Tabernacle Baptist Church in Houston. Inspired by her mother who saw to it that Mary Kay was in Sunday school every week, Mary Kay made the church an important part of her life. (Even today, Mary Kay Ash is tirelessly active in Baptist church activities to which it is reported she donates 10 percent of her income.)

While a sales representative for Stanley Home Products, Mary Kay made up her mind that she could achieve the annual award of Queen of Sales, a feat she soon accomplished. In 1953, after several years of success with Stanley Home Products, she joined World Gifts, a direct sales company headquartered in Houston, and made $1,000 a month in her first year. Before the year was out, she had been promoted to area manager, then national training director which kept her traveling throughout the United States most of the year.

At World Gifts, I found myself teaching men how to do what I did and then they put a man above me to tell *me* what to do, and paid me one-half as much as the male sales managers. Things came to a head when I proposed an audio-visual training program which would cost $35,000 and they told me it was unaffordable. They were afraid I might leave and take part of the company with me and so proposed that I be a national training manager, spending six months in each major city to develop a territory and then move on to another one for another six months. This would have wrecked my family life, so I resigned with a lot of bitterness in my heart. God must have been smiling on me, as I sat down and wrote for two weeks about all the good things that World Gifts had done, to try to get rid of my bitterness.

After two weeks of writing, Mary Kay had constructed a long list of problems confronting women in business.

I firmly believe that in the early sixties God needed someone who believed in femininity and upheld the vision of women being women, and not burning their bras, putting on flat shoes, and trying to emulate the only people who were successful, namely MEN! God used me as a tool to start something He wanted done. This was the propulsion that kept me from doing anything else but what I knew I had to do.

Since 1953 Mary Kay had been using a skin-cream product that was derived from a basic substance used in the tanning of skins and hides. Her own skin had responded in a remarkable way. (Today, her skin appears as fresh and young as that of a twenty year-old.) In 1963 she bought the formula from the grand-daughter of its original developer, and with $5,000 of starting capital began 'Beauty by Mary Kay' in a 500-square-foot store-front in Dallas. Her staff was her second husband (who died of a heart attack while the business was starting up) and nine "beauty consultants," four of whom are still with the company.[2] First year sales were $198,000, and after racking up $800,000 in the second year, the company moved to larger quarters. By that time, she had brought her son Richard Rogers, then age twenty, into the business. Another son, Ben Rogers, also joined the business but didn't stay with it.

Richard had two years at the University of North Texas and has been a tower of strength to me over the years. He has always handled the financial and administrative side of the business, so I don't have to bother my head about it. I handle all matters relating to sales and people. We have never had an argument in twenty-three years. It's been a wonderful relationship to be able to talk to one's son any hour of the day. We are perfect partners.

Two years after the sudden death of her second husband, Mary Kay married Mel Ash, a relationship that lasted for fifteen happy years until death from cancer came to Mel. Mary Kay was filled with grief at his passing, but leaned heavily on her deep religious faith during this critical time of her life. As she expressed it in her autobiography, "When you lose a loved one through death, you must know that person is in a better place; your grief is really for yourself. Life is for the living and we must carry on."

The company has spent the last five years researching skin care. The Dallas facility has a laboratory of white-coated scientists devoted to researching the latest developments in the industry. "Here we feel we are at the top of the ladder," claims Mary Kay. "Recently, we reorganized our line with complete, new products. While there is no 'magic formula' for skin care, we've got the very latest in scientifically researched new products."

Once each year, the company presents a "Pageant Night," to which are invited the outstanding beauty consultants of the entire organization to receive prizes consisting of fur coats, diamond jewelry, and pink Cadillacs. The atmosphere on Pageant Night is electric and has been described as a "cross between a Las Vegas revue and a revival meeting. Hands reach up to touch Mary Kay; a pink Cadillac revolves on a mist-shrouded pedestal; a fifty-piece band plays; and women sob."[3] In *Mary Kay on People Management*, Mary Kay urges managers to "praise people to success," and she does not take the maxim lightly.[4] Her consultants, from the most lowly to the most exalted, receive tremendous recognition. Monthly prizes are mailed to their homes. Each consultant gets a card on her birthday, and top performers are listed in Mary Kay's monthly magazine, aptly called *Applause*.

The key to success in the direct-selling field lies in a company's ability to recruit people who can recruit others. Mary Kay consultants want to be recruiters because it is by bringing in other consultants that they earn bonuses. The recruiting bonus does not come out of the recruit's earnings, but is paid directly from the home office. After six months, a consultant can begin to qualify for a directorship and all its "perks," such as the famous pink Cadillacs. The marketing concept is simple: in order to make $500, a consultant must sell $1,000 worth of Mary Kay products. She builds her clientele by offering free trial facials, usually given in the client's home. The product line has expanded into hair care, body care, and fragrance, but nearly 50 percent of total sales stems from the original skin-care system developed by the legendary hide tanner.

Mary Kay Ash maintains that "our most important asset doesn't appear on our balance sheet. It's our *people* that represent our most valuable asset." She lists the company priorities as

"God first, family second, job third," and when asked to explain it, she will point out that women need the spiritual strength that comes from faith in a greater power and that all women should be free to put their family life first above all other commitments. She especially understands the working mother's plight and points to the great advantage of being a Mary Kay consultant. "This is a job that is compatible with motherhood. You can make $30,000 a year and still be home when the kids get off the school bus!"

Mary Kay Cosmetics, Inc. became a public company in 1968, with its stock listed on the New York Stock Exchange. After a 2-for–1 split at a high of $44 per share in 1983, the stock sunk from $22 to a low of $9 per share in 1984, due mainly to a slump in consultant recruitment which deteriorated the company's sales and profits. In 1985 Mary Kay and her managers decided to make the company private by offering shareholders $11 in cash per share plus subordinated debentures that would mature to $8.25 over five years. By this offering to shareholders at a price higher than the market price, Mary Kay Cosmetics became a privately owned company again. The financial transaction, which involved increasing the debt structure of the company by $141 million, was handled by Morgan, Stanley and Company and the Bank of New York. The latter made a loan of $81 million, with Morgan, Stanley underwriting $60 million in bonds through private placements. "We've solved all of our recruiting problems by being more aggressive," related Mary Kay Ash. "Our sales are running well ahead of last year and we're heading right back up to the top of the mountain. I can still hear my mother saying, 'You can do it, honey.' "

NOTES

1. Mary Kay Ash, *Mary Kay* (New York: Harper & Row, 1981), p. 113.

2. Ibid., p. 57.

3. Kim Wiley, "Cold Cream and Hard Cash," *Savvy*, June 1985.

4. Mary Kay Ash, *Mary Kay on People Management* (New York: Warner Books, 1984), p. 21.

11

MARYLES CASTO

Never Say No

Maryles Casto

Maryles Casto runs a top travel agency with three offices in the San Francisco area. Her business, which she began in 1974 with a $1,500 investment, currently grosses over $40 million annually and has 104 employees, mostly women. In spite of her affluent background in the Philippines where she grew up in a family served by chauffeurs and maids—her father was a well-to-do Filipino plantation owner—Maryles learned what it's like to start from the bottom at $600 a month, working for a San Francisco travel agency.

One of seven children—she was the fourth—her early schooling was in a private school in Celus, the Philippines, followed by a short stint at a woman's college in Manila, before she joined Philippine Airlines as a flight attendant at the age of eighteen. Casto recalls that during her teenage years she saw herself as a person who was "different." "I was always the class leader—always looking for new projects and trying to do better. I think my mother was the most important influence in my life at that time. She always said, 'If you want to accomplish something, you *can* do it.' My father only *thought* he ruled the household; it was my mother who pulled us all together." Her life of affluence in the Philippines was seen by her as "useless," a life that failed to prepare her for living in America where she had to learn the basics of cooking, cleaning, sewing, and shopping. Casto credits her husband Mar Dell Casto, a real estate developer, for teaching her these basics, although she still regards her six-year service as a flight attendant as one of the most important phases of her education. "It was sort of like a finishing school," she relates. "I learned how to dress smartly, how to walk, how to please customers, and above all, I learned the important things a travel agent should know, but many do not."

Maryles met her husband on a blind date while he was a U.S. Army officer. "I first saw a gorgeous picture of him as a scuba diver and remember saying 'WOW!' When I eventually got to meet him, I decided he was mine!" The Castos have an eleven-year-old son and a comfortable life in their home in San Jose.

Maryles, who visits all three offices on a rotating basis, and can call each of her 104 employees by their first names, gives her family top priority, especially her son Mark, making sure she's home at 6:00 P.M. to spend time with him before dinner each day.

Casto started in the travel agency business after she married. "I wanted to stay with the airline, but in those days you couldn't if you were married." Her first job was with Travel Planners, a medium-size agency in San Jose. The owner, John Sell, provided her with the opportunity to learn. "He actually taught me a lot but didn't pay me a salary that was equal to the men in the agency," recalls Casto who claims that *service* is the secret of success in the travel business.

I'm an Oriental and in the Orient, they anticipate your needs well in advance. When I worked for Travel Planners, I found this lacking—everybody was ready to say "no." I believe one should never say "no" or "can't" without trying first to find a solution. I decided to have my own business because I wanted to show what service is all about—ultimate service—I'm a perfectionist in this area. I make sure my employees thoroughly understand what happens when traveling by conducting seminars and organized tours to airports to see what goes on behind the scenes—such as food service, baggage checking—so they will know everything about booking reservations.

Casto opened her business in October 1974, in the midst of a recession, and started making money immediately. "My partner—who invested $1,500 with me—handled individual personal accounts and I went after corporate accounts, calling on firms in Silicon Valley, knowing I had something to offer. Soon I had acquired as clients Signetics, Intel Corporation, A. T. & T., and Rohm Corporation. My clients were typical entrepreneurs: high-pressure, quick-paced, very demanding—everything needed at the last minute." One start-up company she remembers vividly had just a hundred employees and a dream to build personal computers. "It had the strange name of Apple Computer," she relates with a wide grin. "Also, much of the success of our agency comes from cultivating friendships with executive secretaries. They are the ones who decide which agency will be used."

In 1976 Maryles bought out her partner's 50 percent interest. Casto Travel has had constant growth since its very beginning and the agency now ranks in the top 10 percent of the nation's independent travel agencies.

In spite of Maryles Casto's limited experience in management, she seems to have overcome it by combining a lot of enthusiasm and energy with a keen sense of the human side of enterprise. "I had no real management background when I started Casto Travel, but I was always able to put myself in the other person's place. I learned this from both my parents who brought us up to understand the importance of the Golden Rule." Casto Travel has a remarkably low turnover rate which Maryles attributes to treating her staff "like I want to be treated." "I pay my people a lot—we are one of the highest paid agencies in the business. I expect them to give a lot and I compensate them accordingly." Other innovative benefits keep turnover low among her predominantly female staff. Two part-time employees share one job. New mothers can regain their positions after a year's maternity leave, two months of it with pay. "I'm hoping to start a day-care center in one of my offices. I've got seven pregnant women in my office right now and I want to keep them and put their kids in a nursery right here in the office!" she states. Casto also offers a profit-sharing plan to all her employees.

Maryles Casto claims to have a keen intuitive sense in decision making. "I can smell a situation. My gut feelings regulate most of my decisions—and I try to teach my staff to make full use of their intuitive powers in making decisions." She also exhibits an extraordinary self-confidence and confesses that she never had a fear of failure, attributing this to her mother, as well as her husband who continues to tell her, "Maryles, there's nothing you can't do!"

With offices in San Francisco, Palo Alto, Santa Clara, and a fourth planned for Milpitas, Maryles Casto is planning on grossing $100 million within five years. She has already expanded her interests to the women's fashion field and owns a 51 percent interest in a New York couture company. She recently announced plans to open a travel agency school, to be located in San Francisco, that will provide training for anyone interested in entering the expanding travel industry. Responding to the question "What drives Maryles Casto?", she replied, "Certainly not money. I have a personal commitment to all the people who work for me, including many who started with me. We created a really good company and my responsibility is to see that we stay on the right path."

12

LANE NEMETH

Learning Should Be Fun

Lane Nemeth

Discovery Toys, a $50 million direct-marketing enterprise in the San Francisco Bay Area, is the result of the efforts of a dedicated, determined woman who knows what it's like to live on food stamps. Lane Nemeth started her business in a garage in 1977. Frustrated by a fruitless search of toy stores for high-quality educational toys she knew were available at schools and day-care centers, she planned to start a retail toy store of her own. Both her husband and her father, a retired professional salesman, suggested she consider direct selling—"something like Tupperware." Nemeth pulled a few friends together for a "house party" demonstration of her idea. From this, she readily saw that true, educational toys require demonstration, and with a flash of intuition, a new concept for marketing educational toys was born.

Nemeth knew that educational toys were available through school-supply houses since she had been at one time a day-care center director. Pooling $50,000 of loans from friends and relatives, she ordered enough inventory for projected sales of $100,000 the first year. This turned out to be a big mistake, for her entire stock was sold out by October and the company faced Christmas with plenty of orders and no inventory. The following year, Nemeth made the opposite mistake and over bought, finding herself with $100,000 worth of unsold toys after Christmas and suppliers pressing for payment of bills. "My background was that of a teacher, not a business person, so I then did a dumb thing! I found a loan shark and borrowed $100,000 at 27.5 percent interest." By June of the following year, Nemeth was dead broke again. Fortunately Discovery Toys was rescued from bankruptcy by the New York venture capital firm of Weiss, Peck & Greer which, impressed by Nemeth and her concept, invested $90,000 in Discovery Toys in exchange for 18 percent equity interest. Weiss, Peck & Greer also helped Nemeth secure a $250,000 SBA loan. By 1981, with sales expanding at a rate above plans, the company ran short of working capital again, but tenacious Lane Nemeth talked a local banker into a $250,000 loan.

Then in 1982, Discovery Toys, with sales booming, encountered another cash flow problem, but Nemeth was able to convince a competing bank to grant a $1 million loan, thus providing Discovery Toys with a comfortable financial cushion for the first time in its existence.

In 1983 sales continued to expand, but Nemeth's company had another major crisis—this one caused by a computer failure, resulting in Discovery's inability to deliver thousands of orders by Christmas. Everyone was irate, particularly the "educational consultants" who depended on sales commissions for their livelihood. Acting upon the advice of Mary Kay Ash of Mary Kay Cosmetics, whom Nemeth had befriended, Discovery Toys invested $2 million in an IBM computer with an automated order system called Robo-Pic. The system handles all orders, accounts receivable, sales planning, and other financial applications. It also activates a system of conveyor belts that automatically fill up to 800 orders an hour and, in consequence, it has paid for itself several times over in labor cost reductions.

Discovery Toys' marketing staff conducts roughly 250,000 home demonstrations a year. The staff consists of some 15,000 "educational consultants"—mostly women with professional backgrounds in areas such as teaching, nursing, occupational therapy, or psychology—who love to supplement their incomes by providing toy demonstrations in parents' homes. Most are parents themselves and college-educated and thus make up a sales staff that conveys a high caliber of quality and integrity. They go through a standard two-day training session and the company hosts monthly seminars around the country, plus a national convention twice a year.

Consultants are rewarded not only for the actual taking of orders, but, more importantly, for recruiting new consultants. Additional incentives, built on the Mary Kay Cosmetics program, include fur coats, diamond rings, vacations for two, and white Chrysler New Yorkers. Asked about the long-range sales goals for Discovery Toys, Lane Nemeth states that, while she doesn't know how big the market is, she will not rest until the company is doing $1 billion a year. "I get discouraged when I see the market absorbing hundreds of millions of dollars worth of high-priced laser guns and war toys. We want to present toys from which kids can really *learn* something. Our focus is on new product development. We need toys that are parent-interactive as well as child-centered."

The bulk of Discovery Toys' product line sell for under $10. The line includes items for infants and children up to eleven years old, and is confined to ninety items, with some sixty new ones introduced each year as others are withdrawn. Products are designed "in house" and are manufactured elsewhere, mainly in Europe and Japan. The toys must be constructed to withstand the hazards of breakage from dropping, smashing, and biting and, at the same time, must be intellectually stimulating, aesthetically appealing, and safe for children.

Lane Nemeth was born and raised in New York City. While a teenager in high school, her family moved to South Orange, New Jersey, an affluent community where Lane found herself very much a "loner." "My father was the greatest influence in my life. He was the sales vice-president of a photography firm— charming, warm, and handsome—I loved him," relates Nemeth. "My mom was like my sister with whom I fought continuously, and in those days, I really didn't know who I was, except I knew I was smart." Lane Nemeth reached college age at a time when every college and university could pick and choose its students from a long list of applicants. "I got into the University of Pittsburgh on a fluke," says Nemeth. "My grades were not so hot, except for English where I had an SAT score of 800. I was turned down everywhere but Pitt was looking for male students with an English rather than a science bias, and their Admissions Department thought I was a male, because of my name—so they accepted me, not discovering their error until it was too late!" After graduating from Pitt, Nemeth did a master's in education at Seton Hall University, South Orange, New Jersey.

Lane and Ed Nemeth met when they were seventeen years old at a summer camp. They married four years later, and while Ed was doing his master's in physics at the University of Oregon, the new bride couldn't find a job, except for one as a social worker at $1.30 an hour. "Believe it or not, times were so tough we had to apply for food stamps," she recalls. In the years before she started Discovery Toys, Lane had eight different jobs—all of them menial.

I found myself angry most of the time. The only boss whom I respected was one who said "Let me know when you need help and I'll be there to help." That's the kind of boss I am. I allow my managers to do their own things and wait for them to come to me if they need help. Still, I've always had the awareness of the possibility of failure and if it weren't for my child, I'd be in the office nights and weekends. Because of my daughter, Tara, I try to be home by six and never work weekends.

Lane Nemeth has a very special relationship with her daughter, who has first priority on Lane's time. "When our business started, I tried out all the new items on her. She's traveled with me, been on stage with me since she was three years old, and at age twelve, really understands the business." Tara accompanies her mother to Discovery Toys' conventions where she often goes on stage to demonstrate an item to the attending educational consultants. "I travel with Tara as much as I can," says Nemeth. "Quite frankly, I think children can learn more out of school than in school and Tara has already seen Alaska, Mexico, Hawaii, and many other states of the U.S."

When Lane has to travel alone, her husband takes over at home. "I have an exceptional husband," she states with glowing pride. "I met him when I was seventeen, we married at twenty-one, and we are sort of the same person. Ed and I have given Tara a lot of self-confidence and I think the amount of time we spend with her has done this. She fully intends to take over the business someday!"

Asked about the business problems related above, Nemeth recalls how depressed she became in 1983 when things looked so bleak for the company.

We had sales of $10 million and lost over $600,000 due to bad planning—this following a 15 percent pretax profit the year before. When I saw the 1983 financial statement, I thought it was the end. This put me in shock. I came home and said to my husband, "I think we're out of business." I went to bed that night and when I woke in the morning, I questioned my ability for the first time. Then I realized there were a lot of people working for me—depending on the company for their income—and I took inventory of my options:

1. Accept an offer from a large company we had at that time.
2. Wind up the business.
3. Carry on.

I didn't have the audacity to quit, didn't want to sell out, and when I thought of the hundreds of people who depended on me, there was only one option—carry on.

And carry on Nemeth did. Things got better following the introduction of more sophisticated inventory controls, and the business became profitable again. "I learned a lot from this," says Nemeth. "I learned how to correct mistakes quickly, to establish better controls, and develop a keener intuitive insight about the business." Nemeth confesses, however, that her greatest shortcoming is one that is typical of most entrepreneurs, namely the tendency to "fall in love" too quickly. "On hiring people, I'm the worst person I ever met. I will fall in love rapidly with new people and ideas—I like almost everybody—and that's not a good way to hire people. If people are warm, I can't even spot the phoneys."

The financial side of Discovery Toys is now handled by a controller whom Nemeth describes as a "genius." It has been reported that an adversarial relationship developed between Nemeth and Weiss, Peck & Greer during the problems of 1983.[1]

Greer would like Discovery Toys to go public in order to achieve a capital gain on their investment, but Lane Nemeth dismisses the idea. "I'd rather go out of business than sell. I've got everything I need, and so does my family. I will never take my business public; it doesn't make sense. Mary Kay Ash did it and later on went private again. My proudest achievement is the positive role model and secure home life that I have been able to provide for my daughter, while fully exploring my own creative potential. It's been equally satisfying to know that so many other women in Discovery Toys are achieving the same success in their lives. Many of them make over $100,000 per year."

NOTE

1. Michele Beckey, "Information for Business Owners and Entrepreneurs," *Working Woman*, August 1985, p. 39.

13

PAMELA SCURRY

"I Think It's Okay to Want It All"[1]

Pamela Scurry

Pamela Scurry, mother of two at age forty and married to an executive of New York's Chemical Bank, appears to be on her way to having it all for herself and her family. She emphasizes "family" because her version of "having it all" underscores the rich family life she enjoys.

In 1977, with $10,000 borrowed from a bank, Pamela started Wicker Garden, a shop on Manhattan's upper Madison Avenue decorated with white wicker furniture which she loves to collect. In the start-up days, Pam and her husband would cover auction sales and flea markets in the New York area on weekends, purchasing antique wicker to be resold to well-to-do East Side residents and decorators. As the business grew and prospered, she expanded her space to the storefront next door and eventually across the street to a large facility that retails an upscale collection of children's clothes called Wicker Garden's Children. Her first out-of-town store opened in Dallas during the summer of 1987, and Pamela expects Wicker Garden to exceed a $15 million sales mark by 1989.

Scurry considered herself a kind of "outsider" during her early school days. Although she was on a lot of school committees and a cheerleader, she never felt part of the young crowd; nor was she a star student. Due to her father's death when Pamela was thirteen, it was necessary for her to work after school—and now at age forty, she hasn't stopped working. "Although my father was in the insurance business, incredibly he had practically no insurance on his own life and my mother had to work just to pay off the terrible bills accumulated from my father's long illness. Both my parents were extraordinarily ethical and I'm grateful for that, because I developed a keen sense of ethics from them, which is so important in business."

The entrepreneurial spirit was demonstrated by Pamela when she was a mere teenager. Having an innate sense of style, she began making copper enamel jewelry which she sold to boardwalk shops in Atlantic City. She also worked in a florist shop to accumulate enough funds to finance her future college education. Due to her skimpy budget, Scurry enrolled in Oswego State College where tuition costs were comparatively low.

I had a good record at Oswego—captain of the cheerleader squad and held a number of student offices and had the goal of eventually becoming an elementary school teacher. However, without a master's degree this was impossible, so I found an opportunity of entering a special program at Boston College and got my master's degree in twelve months. Fortunately, I had selected computer education as my thesis, so when I graduated, Digital Equipment Company hired me and sent me all over the country for two years as a specialist in computer applications to education.

Scurry didn't find life on the road lonely in those years. She is the kind who makes friends easily and describes her two years "on the road" as "fabulous." In 1971 she was hired away from Digital Equipment by a firm in Silicon Valley, California, that appointed her a vice-president with the responsibility of developing computer systems for schools throughout the state. "At age twenty-five, to be an officer in a corporation made me feel pretty good about myself," says Scurry. "However, I began to sense that the company was indulging in some highly unethical practices, and with the value system I had inherited from my parents, I knew I had to leave—and leave I did just before the company went into bankruptcy."

Pamela Scurry claims to look at most activities as learning experiences—even the distasteful ones like that reported above—so, undaunted in spirit, she returned to New York. After a very short period of unemployment, she was hired by the publishing firm Harcourt Brace Jovanovich as an editor of educational books. After two years, she was promoted to executive editor.

Almost all of Harcourt's executives were male, and somewhat chauvinistic, so I had to get my promotion on the basis of talent. Nevertheless, I could see I was at a dead end so I applied for a job with McKinsey and Company, a leading management consulting firm. After twelve interviews, I was certain I had the job, but after the thirteenth interview, I learned they were not going to hire me and I went home and cried!

It wasn't long after this episode that Pamela began to think of starting a business of her own. Meanwhile, she had met and married Richard Scurry, an IBM executive ten years her senior. "Richard had been a bachelor in New York City for a long time and dated many women until I came along. We had a rather tough time in the first year of our marriage, as Richard and I both had difficulty adjusting to each other's ways." But adjust they did. With two young children and a Fifth Avenue penthouse apartment glowing with antique wicker, the Scurrys now live a life filled with a host of interesting friends. Their children are enrolled in private schools and they vacation as a family, spending July in a rented, ancient Italian castle.

Pamela's entry into the entrepreneurial life after five years working for Harcourt Brace was the result of a spur-of-the-moment decision to buy a shop that was going out of business on upper Madison Avenue. The Scurrys didn't have the necessary ready cash to provide the $10,000 purchase price, so Pamela took out a bank loan and thereby jumped into the antique wicker furniture business. Her husband helped her paint the store's interior a striking white and apple green, and six weeks later Wicker Garden made its debut. Two years later, after her son, and before her daughter, was born, she announced the opening of Wicker Garden's Baby next door. Here are sold cradles, carriages, nursery draperies, and up-scale nursery crib sheets and comforters for babies. Scurry decided when she was eight months pregnant that there were no really good stores specializing in baby clothes. As she explains it, "So I opened a baby department in the adjoining building and the store has grown with them. This gave me the clue to what would be the future growth area of my business." Today, three quarters of her total sales are in baby and children's apparel.

Pam's husband Richard, after nineteen years with IBM, has recently joined Chemical Bank as a vice-president. "He relishes my success and is proud of me," says Pamela. "I manage to swing my family life effectively, I think. My children, Richardson and Kristina, have fun coming in the store and I always allow them to express their opinions on the merchandise selection— and I find this very helpful." As for much of her decision making, Pamela makes full use of her intuitive powers.

My decision to quit my job and start a business came as sort of a flash of intuition. I'm very much right-brained and use both intuition and logic at all times. This has been useful in *sensing* opportunities. Although I've learned to read financial statements without any formal training in bookkeeping or accounting, I don't bother to balance my checkbook; I just *know* what's there. Sometimes I think I'm a witch or maybe a psychic!

Asked about future plans for the growth of Wicker Garden, Scurry told me she hopes to build a network of upper-end children's stores and eventually do her own manufacturing. "We are seeing a swing toward the return of elegance and more conservative American life-styles—even Victorian looks that fit the antique wicker concept," says this entrepreneurial woman who was elected *Retailer of the Year* in 1986 by the New York Chamber of Commerce.

Pamela Scurry's concluding remarks in my interview with her accentuate her outlook on her life as a wife, mother, and entrepreneurial person: "I *do* want it all—but that's just for me and my family. What I have chosen is not for everyone. I think women should have choices but, given *my* choice, I want to be able to be a happy example for choosing it all."

NOTE

1. Mary Finch Hoyt, "Six Women Who Changed Their Lives," *Good Housekeeping*, March 1986, p. 86.

14

ROSE TOTINO

The Loving Queen of Pizza

Rose Totino

Rose Totino, at age seventy-three, is the first woman to be appointed vice-president of the Pillsbury Company, an old-line Minnesota flour-milling concern that has expanded through acquisitions of brand-name processed-food companies. Some of its better known brands are Burger King, Häagen-Dazs, Bennigan's, Green Giant, Jeno's, and Mrs. Totino's Pizzas. The story of Rose Totino, however, is remarkable in Pillsbury's corporate history, for it embodies an account of the typical American success saga—the child of illiterate immigrant parents who created an innovative product, struggled through and overcame incredible obstacles, and with the boundless faith, persistence, and self-confidence of the typical entrepreneur achieved riches and esteem, and now indulges in generous giving to worthy causes.

Pedro and Armita Cruciani, Rose Totino's parents, immigrated to America in 1910 and settled in Old Forge, Pennsylvania, where Pedro got a job digging coal in the anthracite mines of that region. Armita's sister had moved farther west to settle in Minneapolis, and in 1914 the Crucianis followed her there where Pedro found work with the city, paving streets with tar in summer and shoveling snow in winter. The middle of seven children, Rose's life was far from affluent but there was much love and warmth in the family, and Armita managed her brood with both affection and authority. "My mother was a perfectionist," says Rose, "very prim and proper. This was a contrast to my father, a poetic person—loved his wine, loved to sing, a truly carefree character. I loved them and I got a well-balanced childhood direction from both."

Rose's early childhood was filled with work and austerity. As Rose relates it:

Dad had all he could do to make the mortgage payments. Our clothes were made by my mother from flower sacks, and our evening meal was one plate of porridge, or pasta and peas. Then on Saturday—when Dad got paid—we got a little piece of meat. On Sundays, my mother would kill a chicken—we had our own chickens and a cow in the backyard. However, we couldn't afford to drink the cow's milk, and sold it in the neighborhood for five cents a quart. It was my job to peddle the milk. I also had a lemonade stand on hot summer days and got five cents a drink.

With seven children to watch over, Armita Cruciani managed to keep her house clean, her garden growing, her children clothed, and her family fed. Three days of the week were bread-making days and Rose would hurry home from school on these days to wash the big pan her mother used for kneading the dough. Bread-making day also meant a treat for the Crucianis, for Armita would reserve enough dough to make thin-crust pizzas for everyone, and would sprinkle them with sugar and cinnamon. It was the only dessert the family could afford.

Rose quit school after tenth grade, and at the age of sixteen got a job doing housework for $2.50 a day. She recalls: "My older sister had a similar job, so we were able to bring home together $5.00 per week, and that was almost enough to feed our whole family. My two brothers stayed in school because my mother wanted them to get educated—she felt that we girls didn't need an education, claiming that God put us on this earth to be wives and mothers."

Rose was nineteen when she met and began a courtship with Jim Totino, six years her elder, a young man of Italian parents who had a job with the federal government's Works Progress Administration. This was in 1934 when President Roosevelt's New Deal had established the WPA agency for the creation of building projects that provided jobs for the swollen ranks of unemployed during the Great Depression. Just prior to their wedding, Jim had begun working in a bakery which, characteristic of all bakeries, required that he work on night shifts. "Jim bought me a $39 wedding ring with his small savings. I was working in a candy factory for thirty-seven cents per hour, and we couldn't afford a honeymoon, but Jim's boss was nice enough to give him the night off on the day we got married," relates Rose.

The marriage of Jim and Rose was blessed with two daughters, and as the children grew older, Rose became involved in her church and community activities. She was a regular at all PTA meetings, and was a den mother to a local Boy Scout troop. At their social and community gatherings, Rose would always bring along those little pizzas her mother used to make as gifts for everyone attending. Soon friends began asking Rose to cater their parties, at which Mrs. Totino's pizzas were always a big hit. Generally speaking, however, pizzas were only a favorite of the large Italian sections in large cities like New York, Boston, and Chicago. Most people in the midwest had never heard of pizzas, and it was not until the GIs returned from Europe after World War II that a market for this delicious Italian dish became evident among all classes of Americans. Rose recalls that

in 1950 Jim and I started looking for a little shop to sell my pizzas, but when we discovered a little place for $85 a month rent, we found we needed $1,500 to buy some equipment. I called the vice-president of the Central Northwestern Bank about a loan to open a pizza place and he said, "Pizza? What's that?" So, I baked a pizza and took it down with me to the bank. He loved it and I got the loan, pledging our three-year old car as collateral.

Rose's newfound friend at the bank was so taken with the idea that he persuaded the president of the bank to pay for a full-page newspaper ad for the grand opening of Totino's Italian Kitchen at 523 E. Central Avenue in northeast Minneapolis. Totino's Kitchen still exists as a popular place for Italian cuisine.

On opening day, people lined up for two blocks. The business grew and flourished and Jim quit his job at the bakery to come and help me. At the end of each day, we'd be too tired to count the cash, so we just put it in an old brown bag. Next morning, I'd take money out to pay the help, the bread man, the milkman, and the meat man—what was left was profit I figured!

Rose is quick to admit that her lack of bookkeeping knowledge has always plagued her. "I was always good at arithmetic in school and can add figures fast—to this day, I don't use a calculator and love doing figures in my head," she says. Further recounting this lack of sophistication about basic accounting, Rose says, "When the bank would call and ask for a cash flow statement, I was puzzled and told them, 'There's no cash flowing around here!' Then they'd start talking about LIFO and FIFO and I thought those were dogs' names! What little we really knew about running a business!''

The mushrooming take-out business of Totino's Kitchen prompted friends and customers to suggest they have their pizzas frozen and sold in neighborhood supermarkets in the Minneapolis area. After conducting a very successful, small market test with their pizzas at the restaurant of Donaldson's Department Store in downtown Minneapolis, the idea seemed like a good one. Rose was even asked to demonstrate the intricacies of pizza making on a local television show.

Their business now was flourishing, and with Rose's tremendous energy and Jim's support in tending the mechanical and equipment side of the business, the Totinos were able to save an average of $5,000 a year. By the early 1960s, they had accumulated $50,000 and Jim, who loved to hunt and fish, began to talk about retiring and enjoying their riches. After all, they had $50,000 in a savings bank and had paid off the mortgage on the house they had bought for $8,000 in the late 1930s. Also, Jim was not in good health, having developed diabetes. However, after much soul-searching, Rose's entrepreneurial spirit, her intense drive, and the taste of success in their enterprise disposed of any further notion of not moving forward with the business.

The Totinos had by this time proven that a market for pizza was here to stay and they started thinking seriously about producing frozen pizza in quantity. In late 1961, they found a location—a former salad-dressing plant. Realizing that producing large quantities would require a bakery with expensive equipment, for which they did not have the financing, a fast-talking advertising person sold Rose on the idea of selling and promoting Mrs. Totino's Frozen Pasta Entrees. The idea sounded good, for Totino's Kitchen had by this time expanded into a restaurant and was becoming known for its manicotti and mastaccioli. The plan was to accumulate enough from the venture to eventually finance a bakery for making Totino's pizzas. Unfortunately, the ad campaign, which cost $80,000, and the entire idea proved to be a failure. The Totinos had begun production in January of 1962, and by August had lost $150,000. Rose describes the picture: "When I told Jim we were actually broke, he said, 'Rosey, we'll just have to file for bankruptcy.' I said I couldn't do that. We owe all those people money and can't stick them. 'Maybe you'll have to go back and work in the bakery,' I told Jim, and 'I'll take in washing—but we've just got to work out of this mess and pay those people back." (The episode characterizes a common failure of marketers having consumer-accepted products who expand product lines before doing sufficient preliminary market research that determines customer reaction. As it turned out, frozen pasta entrees in 1962 were years ahead of their time. Today—thanks to two decades of technical progress in refrigeration and microwave ovens, together with dramatic changes in consumer life-styles—frozen pasta occupies a significant share of the frozen food market).

One weekend, during those dark days for the Totinos, Jim journeyed to a food convention in Dallas and discovered that a Chicago firm was making pizza crusts and selling them to big pizza companies who would pour topping on the crusts and sell them. Rose immediately saw an opportunity. "Maybe we don't need to build that bakery," she told Jim. "Just buy the crusts, fill them with toppings, freeze'em and sell'em."

By this time, Rose had applied for a Small Business Administration loan to try and save the business. Nevertheless, her feelings of depression emanating from the size of the company's debts began to test the deep religious faith that was a heritage of her childhood.

"I was beginning to question God's love," she recalls,

I didn't pray about my problems, but one morning—just as St. Paul had his encounter with the Lord on the road to Damascus—I had mine on Route 100. I was about half a mile from the plant and ran across a station on my car radio where a man was talking about God's love and how he wants everyone to come to Him with problems. At that moment, I gave my whole heart to God, and I said to the Lord, "Help me out of this mess, and I'll spend the rest of my life serving you; just show me the way!" When I got to the plant, the SBA man was there to tell me they had approved our loan. I said to myself, "Oh Lord God, you really work fast!" From that day forward, everything got better, and in the first month in the frozen pizza business we did $100,000 in sales! I said, my gosh, we don't need to make this much money, so I went into the plant and told our production manager to put some extra meat in our pizzas and keep our customers happy!

Over the ensuing years, Mrs. Totino's Pizzas became an accepted brand in many areas of the United States. Food brokers introduced the product to supermarkets in regions outside of the Minneapolis area. By 1970 the Totinos knew they needed larger facilities to supply the demand for their product. Their bank financed a new, modern plant in Fridley, a north Minneapolis suburb, and Rose went to work to build an executive team. Her principal support in this area came from Joe Desnick, a food broker who had placed her products in every major supermarket in his territory. As Rose recounts it, "Joe knew a lot about food marketing. He helped me hire people—in fact, we even hired his own assistant away from him, Ron Miley." Ron was made head of marketing and later became the president of the company. According to a biographical sketch of Rose Totino that appears in a publication about twelve outstanding Minnesota entrepreneurs, Miley is quoted as having stated: "Around Rose you have a feeling that things are going to work out. Just about everyone who worked there feels it was the best place we've ever worked. We'd do it again in a minute."[1]

Rose Totino's great concern about the people who work in her plant is seen in the fact that the employees have no union representation; an unusual phenomenon in the food-processing business. Says Rose, "We've seen many attempts by unions to come in but my employees are all my friends—they don't need a union."

Another major player in the thriving frozen pizza business of the early 1970s was Jeno's Pizzas of Duluth, Minnesota. "Jeno started his business five years after me," relates Rose. "He was a male chauvinist and didn't think much of women running businesses—even claimed that he would 'bury me.' Ever since he said that, it was a tough competitive battle between the two of us. He was bigger than we were and spent more than we did on promotions. Although Jeno never spoke kindly about me, I never bad-mouthed him and it was good that I followed my mother's advice to never speak ill of anyone because it would have come back to haunt me—since Pillsbury now owns Jeno's!"

By the mid-seventies, Mrs. Totino's Pizzas, Inc. was racking up an annual sales volume of $37 million. Some of the major food-processing companies such as Pillsbury, General Mills, Heinz, Stouffer's, and Sara Lee were all interested in acquiring the Totino business. Jim's health problems with diabetes were exacerbated with Parkinson's disease, and not having any sons to take over, the Totinos decided to accept an offer from the Pillsbury Company for $22,190,000 in shares of that firm's stock. William Spoor, Pillsbury's then chief executive, asked Rose—as a condition of the deal—to remain with the company and become the first woman vice-president of this 107-year-old Minnesota company. (I was recently told by a senior executive of the Pillsbury Company that at the formal closing of the Totino merger all the usual contracts and documents of the deal were signed. Then, everyone stood up, shook hands, and congratulated each other, and Rose and Jim departed, leaving the $22,190,000 worth of Pillsbury shares on the conference room table!)

Jim Totino, to whom Rose wistfully refers as "my Jim," passed away in 1981 and Rose continued with the company, as she does today, in the capacity of quality control director and chief of public relations for Mrs. Totino's Frozen Pizza Division of the Pillsbury Company. Sales in her division have grown to a figure in excess of $200 million, as Rose maintains a close personal relationship with some fifty food brokers who market her product nationwide, as well as in Canada, Japan, and West Germany. Every eighteen months, she takes a group of brokers—winners of sales competitions—and their wives to Italy. The junket includes a day-long party in the village where her mother was born; the villagers serve them local food dishes and homemade wine, and the village band plays while everyone dances. According to Richard Nickel, the vice-president of marketing, "at the end of the day, there are tears in everyone's eyes."[2]

Rose Totino's office in her Fridley, Minnesota, plant is tastefully furnished to resemble a combination Italian kitchen and pizza parlor, complete with red gingham curtains and accessories. Pots and pans hang from the ceiling and Rose thinks nothing of personally whipping up here—in her office—a seven-course meal for her business guests.

Describing her current role with Pillsbury, Rose says, "I love to cook and I love people. And I love to feed people. That's how it all started—cooking at home, making pizzas for family and friends. Our standard here is excellence. We are going to be the best pizza company in the world, and we've got a team that, believe me, will make it happen."

Her intense religious faith and love shines through in all her dealings with people, not only with her employees and business associates, but strangers on first meeting. One discerns upon visiting with her for a little while that in her charitable activities, her abundant giving returns to her tenfold. The personal commitment she made to her Lord—on Route 100 in April of 1965—is certainly not forgotten, for she has since given a total of $14 million through her foundation to numerous charities. When I asked her what she would wish to have inscribed on her tombstone, she replied that when her time comes, she would like it to state the following: "All I ask of you is that you will forever remember me as loving you."

NOTES

1. Carol Pine, and Susan Mundale, *Self-Made* (Minneapolis, Minn.: Dorn Books, 1982,) p. 154.
2. Ibid., p. 158.

15

DOROTHY BRUNSON

Revolutionary of Radio

Dorothy Brunson

Dorothy Brunson, born in poverty, is well on her way to building a radio-television empire. The owner of three radio stations, she recently won an FCC selection from among six finalists for a license to operate a five-million-watt TV station in the greater Philadelphia area, the fourth largest market in the United States. Brunson is an admitted workaholic and an entrepreneur with a passion for business whose career thus far has given her all the basic skills of management and a strong background in accounting, retailing, and advertising. Her success in radio broadcasting derives from a new creative programming formula that blends the best of traditionally ethnic white and black music. Early in her career in radio, she found that the practice of advertisers of buying radio time for products specifically geared for blacks was becoming outdated. Her research demonstrated that all people, both black and white, at the same economic levels generally purchase goods in a similar way. Using her research, she was able to convince advertisers that there exists a massive interracial audience in the twelve-to-thirty-nine-year-old age group—the very people sought by the advertisers. When Brunson was managing Inner City Broadcasting, her implementation of this formula enabled the company, which owned one daytime radio station in New York (WBLS), to grow into a chain of seven major-market stations grossing annual sales of $23 million.

Dorothy Brunson started her career in broadcasting in 1964, as an assistant controller for station WWRL in New York. Her entrepreneurial career began when she and radio-station colleague Howard Sanders left WWRL to start one of the first black-owned advertising agencies. The business was financed with an initial investment of $25,000 and six months later an SBA loan, but the partnership didn't survive. As she relates, "Howard was charming, talented, and ahead of his time. He could talk fluently in four languages, but had no follow-through. I'm organized, he wasn't; he would be late for important appointments and that drove me crazy." Upon their parting, Sanders agreed to buy Dorothy's interest for $115,000, which she used to open her second enterprise, an apparel store catering to stout women on Harlem's 125th Street. "I would buy overruns from manufacturers of large-size women's coats and dresses and soon realized I had a gold mine," says Brunson. Then disaster struck. Lane Bryant, a multi-store chain specializing in large-size women's apparel, opened a store right next door to hers. "They even told their suppliers not to sell me goods and I tried to sue them, but I soon realized the legal bills would kill me. I even tried to picket them, but that was too time-consuming, so I just said 'to hell with it,' paid off my creditors, and took a big loss."

At this point (1973), Brunson realized that her strength was in broadcasting. One day she got a phone call from a friend who wanted her to invest $15,000 in WLIB, a black-oriented AM station owned by Inner City Broadcasting. She was also asked to put together a group of investors. "I got about eight or nine friends and raised a pool of equity funds totaling $75,000." The infusion of cash was insufficient to relieve the station's financial problems. Six months later, under pressure from the bank that held the start-up loan, Brunson was asked by Inner City to take over the job of general manager. The station was by this time $1 million in debt.

The persistent Dorothy restructured the station, made it more community-oriented, and started paying off the bank a little at a time. Over the next six years, under Brunson's management Inner City acquired six more radio stations and became a thriving, profitable enterprise. But her drive for autonomy and the need to "do her own thing," as she relates it, prompted her to abandon a $100,000 a year salary and purchase the bankrupt radio station WEBB in Baltimore with $85,000 of her own funds, which she had received from her investment in Inner City, and $400,000 financing from Security Pacific Capital Corporation, a California venture capital firm. "I couldn't afford to pay myself a salary for the first two and a half years—and had to change my living standards radically. My mother told me I was crazy to give up $100,000 salary and a nine-room co-op in Manhattan to move into a tiny Baltimore apartment, but I knew in my gut that it would be a success." With an incredible struggle against seemingly insurmountable roadblocks, which included efforts by competing stations to block her FCC license, Brunson has brought WEBB to profitability. In the meantime, she has also acquired station WIGO in Atlanta and WBMS in Wilmington, South Carolina. Her successful quest for a license to operate a new TV station to cover the greater Philadelphia area is her crowning achievement. In my interview with this remarkable woman, she refers to the new venture as a "minnow becoming a whale."

Dorothy Brunson was born in Tattnal, Georgia, in 1938, and shortly thereafter moved with her parents to New York's Harlem. Her father died when Dorothy was a child and her mother later remarried and worked as a laundress to help support the family. "There was never any doubt in my mind when I was a child in Harlem that I wanted to make money," recalls Brunson.

When people would say "What do you want to be when you grow up?," I would say "rich." I really didn't become intellectually awakened until my teens. I was a lousy student in my first six or seven years of school and was really angry at the world. After eighth grade, I became good in math and science. I was always competitive and very clear about the fact that I did not want to remain poor. I was always looking for something—read a lot and spent hours in the library. I loved to read stories about people who had succeeded.

Brunson's role model as a teenager was civil rights pioneer Mary McLeod Bethune, a child of former slaves who fought through an impoverished childhood in South Carolina and eventually founded the Florida college that bears her name.

Here was a woman who had no social environment nor network contacts to help her, and no money, yet she built a college. I began to believe that Mary Bethune was right in claiming that the barrier for black people is not so much color as it is economics, and if you've got the bucks, color vanishes. So I made up my mind to get the bucks.

Brunson went through New York's High School of Industrial Arts where she concentrated on advertising art. For a year and half, she attended Tennessee State University in Nashville, but was not a serious student. Eventually, she decided to take courses that could help her make some money, and returning to New York, took courses in accounting, finance, and economics at Pace College and Empire State College, which she financed from her salary as an office temporary. "While I worked as an office temporary as a bookkeeper, I began to develop a reputation as a good accountant," she relates. Soon she got a job full time in a radio station as a bookkeeper and moved up swiftly to assistant controller, then controller where she had to deal with bankers. She relates: "The real value of my accounting courses at college came to me when I had to submit plans to bankers. In business I always tell people, 'Become good friends with your banker, but at the same time befriend another banker or two, in the event you might need to negotiate a better deal.' " Brunson's acquisitions of radio stations have been largely financed with outside loans from both venture capitalists and banks. "Bankers tend—especially with women—to mold the relationship into a kind of protective one. They see themselves as your *guardian* and try to discourage further risk taking," she claims.

Brunson, in spite of her busy schedule that keeps her away from home ten days each month, has managed to raise two sons who are now in college and who work during the summer vacations in their mother's radio stations. Her marriage at age twenty-six was terminated twelve years later and Brunson claims to remain "good friends" with James Brunson, her ex-husband who continues to share in the rearing of their two sons. In the early days of her marriage, when at first she retained her maiden name of Dorothy Edwards, she began to grow in numerous ways at a much faster pace than her husband. "The first time I made more money than he did, he hit the ceiling," she states.

And once someone called him "Mr. Edwards" and his pride was so badly bruised, I decided to become Dorothy Brunson just to keep him happy. James had only an associate college degree and worked for New York's Transit Authority. I used to browbeat him to go back to college, but he was content to stay with his civil service job. I decided I didn't want to live with someone with that little ambition, so we sat down and talked about it and we agreed to separate.

That was in 1976, and Brunson has not remarried.

Her days usually start at 6:00 A.M. at her desk in one of the three radio stations she owns, but Brunson has a great sense of social responsibility, assisting wherever she can in support of the black community. As president of HUB, a Baltimore economic revitalization group of black entrepreneurs, she sees that group as a "first generation of entrepreneurs" who are now in a position to address meaningfully the problems of the black community. Brunson sees the need for changes in attitude of the scores of black youths who are not motivated. As she states it, "The core of the solution is communicating to young people in such a way that they can get to understand that there's more to life than they perceive it." Her HUB group and her activities within her parish church in Baltimore have raised millions of dollars to fund programs and hire trained professional people to work on these problems. Brunson claims their efforts are just now beginning to pay off but expects they will have no real impact until the turn of the century. Her great concern is expressed in her own question, "Can we do it fast enough?"

Dorothy Brunson looks at the future of communications with enthusiastic, hopeful expectations. As she states in her own forecast:

I'm excited about the way telephone and TV will interconnect. I see many new and exciting things out there. The entire process of entertainment is changing fast. While radio will always occupy a portion of the total, the real growth will be in the fields that relate to television. I see an enormous interconnecting of TV with newspapers and I would like, with my new station, to be in the forefront of that. I see great opportunities in the use of video in education. Information is now a bombardment process, so we've got to find a way of dealing with it and can't teach kids the same way we did fifty years ago. I'd like to participate in finding new ways to enhance the learning process.

At age fifty, entrepreneur Dorothy Brunson's achievements are abundant. She ascribes her accomplishments to hard work, "stick-to-itness" (her own phrase), and the self-confidence that comes from many years of experience in her field. When I asked her the question, "What would you most like to be remembered for?", her reply was, "I want to be remembered for the jobs and opportunities I've created for others."

16

ESTÉE LAUDER

High Priestess of Cosmetics

Estée Lauder

I have met Estée Lauder socially on several occasions, and since we have numerous mutual friends and acquaintances, I thought it would be a routine matter to arrange an interview with this most remarkable of all living entrepreneurial women. My request for an interview appointment was answered by her public relations director in a polite note stating Mrs. Lauder's policy to refuse similar requests even from close personal friends because of her autobiography, *Estée: A Success Story.*[1] The note further stated, "I regret that it is not possible for Mrs. Lauder to participate, and hope you understand." I immediately purchased a copy of her book, and after reading it, telephoned a mutual friend who told me I would find a more accurate version of her life in Lee Israel's book, *Estée Lauder: Beyond the Magic.*[2] (Israel had previously published best-seller biographies of Tallulah Bankhead and Dorothy Kilgallen.) After reading Israel's investigative reporting of Estée Lauder's life in a biography that resulted from an abundance of scholarly research, I readily understood why I was rebuffed in my efforts to interview this extraordinary woman.

This chapter, therefore, will provide, in capsule form, a description of the career of Estée Lauder and her successful struggle to the top. I have extracted information from both books. Some accounts of her life as laid down in Lauder's autobiography are in direct contrast with the accounts of her life as written by Lee Israel. Therefore, *both* books should be read by anyone who is interested in learning about the *real* Estée Lauder.

An illustration of this contrast is seen in the introduction of Israel's book which refers to a September 1969 two-page profile of Lauder published in *Women's Wear Daily*, in which Estée told the author of the article that her dreams of achievements in the world of beauty were born when she was twelve years old. Quoting from the interview, the article relates, "She was living with her family in Flushing, Long Island, in a large private house with a stable, a chauffeured car, and an Italian nurse, when she began thinking seriously about becoming a skin doctor." Israel's research has established that Lauder was actually born Josephine Esther Mentzer on July 1, 1908, on Hillside Avenue in Corona, Queens, at home, delivered by a midwife.[3] She was the ninth child of Rose Schotz Rosenthal Mentzer. Max Mentzer was mother Rose's second husband. Rose was born in Hungary and immigrated with six children to New York in 1898 where she married Max Mentzer around 1905. Max had also emigrated from his native Hungary, and when naturalized in 1878 was recorded in the immigration records as being a tailor. By the time Estée entered the world, Max Mentzer had opened a feed-and-grain establishment that later became a hardware store in Corona. His family were among the very few Jewish people in an almost entirely Italian community. Estée attended P.S. 14 in Corona, a few blocks from her father's store, which by this time had expanded into a drygoods operation. According to Israel's account, the family lived over the store. The 1925 New York State Census listed Estée as being "Estella Mentzer" at 172 Corona Avenue. At the age of sixteen, Estée was attending high school, while at the same time gaining merchandising experience at Plafker and Rosenthal, a department store across the street that was owned and operated by Fannie and Frieda Leppel, who were sisters of mother Rose Mentzer.

As a teenager, Estée developed a keen interest in women's fashions. She loved to study cosmetics and particularly the new facial creams that were coming on the market in the mid-twenties. "After school, I would work on my family's faces and hair. Much to the disdain of my straight-laced European parents, I was caught up with American glamour and dreamed of being a skin specialist and making women beautiful," relates Lauder in her autobiography. Her real mentor at this time was her uncle John Schotz, a Hungarian immigrant chemist who had established a laboratory in 1924 where he made simple fragrances. (According to Israel's research, his product line included suppositories, mange cure, paint and varnish remover, toothache remedies, and mustache wax.) Estée describes her Uncle John as a "quiet, bespectacled man who also loved touching faces. He taught me not to use soap and water but to use oils to cleanse, freshen, and moisten the skin." As Lauder reflects on her relationship with John Schotz, she relates: "Uncle John had worlds to teach me . . . and my future was being written in a jar of snow cream." Further, she proclaims philosophically, "In every life there is a moment—an event or a realization—that changes that life irrevocably. If the change is to be a happy one, one must recognize the moment and seize it without delay."[4]

Estée Lauder continued in high school, although there are no accounts of her ultimate graduation in Israel's research of her life. Estée also continued working with her uncle on various types of creams, experimenting and studying their effects on the faces of her family, as well as her high school classmates. At age nineteen, she met Joe Lauter, the son of Hungarian immigrants, and her very first beau. He was twenty-five and had been born and raised on New York's Lower East Side, attended the High School of Commerce, and had studied accounting. He had worked in various businesses, mainly apparel-fabric concerns. Estée and Joe married on January 15, 1930—at the beginning of the Great Depression. Their first child, Leonard Allan Lauter, was born in New York City on March 19, 1933. By 1937, their name had been changed from Lauter to *Lauder*.

Estée continued to experiment with various types of face creams, cooking them in her kitchen. Her intense internal drive soon made her bored with the role of "staying home and playing Mommy." She even undertook a stint at studying acting at New York's Cherry Lane Theater. Lauder relates how young Leonard would "sit in the back row of the theatre and watch as I rehearsed."[5]

Her acting career was short-lived as she soon saw she would never make it to the top of that profession. So Estée started demonstrating and selling her skin creams successfully in beauty salons throughout the New York area. Lauder admits that her intense drive to succeed, coupled with an appetite for social excitement, intimidated her husband. She describes their problems:

We both yearned for success but had very different ways of seeking it. Being young, we were not accomplished in compromise. Deep, deep in my heart I loved him so much, but I was impatient and moving ahead faster than he. Joe was solid and serene. I was quicksilver and driven. . . . For longer and longer periods of time, I was traveling to hotels, leaving Joe at home with Leonard and a maid. I was single-minded in the pursuit of my dream. . . . People were referring to Joe as Mr. Estée Lauder. He didn't like it at all.[6]

Tension at home grew to the breaking point and they divorced in 1939. After the divorce, Estée began traveling to resort areas, selling her creams and giving free facials to women hotel guests, and as her reputation grew, she extended her operation by putting on "in-store" demonstrations in New York and Palm Beach beauty salons and stores. During this time, Estée's intense ambition to elevate her social status drove her to seek and exploit every opportunity to cultivate people with power, wealth, and social prestige. As Israel reports it: "Estée schlepped, hawked, instructed, and cultivated anyone who could help her professionally or socially."[7] One of these was a Dutch-born industrialist, A. I. van Amerigen who later became chief executive officer of International Flavors and Fragrances, the largest creator of fragrances and flavors in America.

By 1943, after four years of separation from Joe Lauder during which she admits to having had close relationships with several men, she returned to her first great love. She and Joe were quietly remarried in December 1943, and in 1944 produced their second child, Ronald Lauder. Reflecting on her divorce and remarriage, Estée makes the touching comment: "During the years I was apart from Joe, in one way I had a heady, exciting time, but I'll always remember coming home at night and not having that one, sweet, trusted someone with whom to share my deep thoughts, my secret. You cannot fly on one wing."[8]

Joe joined in Estée's cosmetic activities, and the first office of Estée Lauder, Inc. opened at 39 East Sixtieth Street in 1945. Estée herself began introducing her products at such stores as Bonwit Teller, Saks Fifth Avenue, and Macy's where much of her time was spent behind the cosmetic counters giving facials to customers as she demonstrated her products and made gifts with purchase, a sales-promotion technique now used by all cosmetic companies. Throughout the decade from the mid-forties to the mid-fifties she traveled to specialty and department stores in every major city in America, promoting the Estée Lauder line. She worked behind counters, trained salespeople on proper selling techniques, and rewarded important store buyers with lavish entertainment. As Lee Israel describes those early years of spectacular growth: "Joe worked from 8 A.M. to 7 P.M., seven days a week. Leonard pitched in whenever he could, delivering goods to Saks Fifth Avenue on his bicycle after school and on Saturdays. He remembers that once during his adolescence, his mother was away for twenty-five continuous weeks!"[9]

The company's big leap forward came in 1953 with the fragrance Youth Dew, first introduced as a bath oil. It was an overnight success and soon came to represent 80 percent of Lauder's total business. (Estée claims that Youth Dew sales in 1984 totaled $150 million worldwide.[10]) This success enabled the Lauders to move from their modest West Side apartment to a townhouse on East Seventieth Street and to embark upon a "tonier" social life that eventually expanded to Palm Beach where Estée purchased a large Georgian mansion and to the south of France where several years later she bought a summer villa.

Other great successes that have helped build Estée Lauder into a worldwide cosmetic empire are products such as Aramis (cologne and aftershave) launched in 1965 and still a major product in the men's fragrance market, and more recently, Lauder for Men and J.H.L., an expensive men's fragrance named after Joe Lauder. In the early seventies, Lauder launched Clinique, a customized line of products created for a younger generation of women to whom beauty products are less of an embellishment and more a part of fitness, health, and good grooming. With so many more women entering the corporate world, the idea had a special appeal. The products were marketed as therapeutic skin care with no reference to the Estée Lauder label. Losses in Clinique totaled $3 million in the first two years, but Estée's extreme persistence continued. Carol Phillips, a former editor of *Vogue* who was hired to run the division, brought it into the black by the late seventies and, according to trade sources, the product line has never stopped growing. (Estée claims its sales were $200 million in 1985.[11])

Today, Leonard Lauder, who is highly respected in the industry, presides over a family business that is approaching sales of $1.5 billion worldwide. Leonard still listens to Estée, who is considered the "Queen Mother" of the Lauder dynasty as she becomes an octogenarian. Joe Lauder died in 1983, and Estée still grieves over the loss of the great love of her life. Her son Ronald left the business for a life of government service, and after a stint in Washington with the Department of Defense, was appointed U.S. Ambassador to Austria, a post he relinquished in 1987.

In Estée Lauder's remarkable career is a dramatic demonstration of the extreme entrepreneurial spirit. Her ambition to succeed *professionally* and *socially* has been the driving force in her life. She constantly strove to overcome all obstacles in her path. She took on her competitors with the sly cunningness of a fox. She captured among her friends and acquaintances members of royalty such as the late Duke and Duchess of Windsor, Princess Grace and Prince Rainier, the Begum Aga Khan, social butterflies like Betsy Bloomingdale and Mrs. Winston Guest, popular celebrities like Bob Hope, Lauren Bacall and Douglas Fairbanks, Jr., and people in the highest levels of government such as the Ronald Reagans, the Gerald Fords, and the Richard Nixons. (President Nixon offered her the ambassadorship to Luxembourg, which she politely rejected.) Being Jewish, she privately observes the traditions of the High Holy Days,[12] but according to Israel's account, she has attempted to avoid being Jewish.[13] Commenting on her religious beliefs, Lauder explains she has an "ecumenical" approach to religion.[14] Her philanthropy is notable, as she has given, through the Estée and Joseph Lauder Foundation, millions of dollars to such agencies as children's parks in New York, the Museum of Modern Art, the Whitney Museum, the Wharton School of Business, and many Jewish charities. Numerous honors have been heaped upon her including France's renowned Legion of Honor.

Josephine Esther Mentzer, born of Hungarian immigrant parents over a store in Corona, Queens, has realized most of her objectives. She built one of the world's largest cosmetic enterprises, developed friendships with the movers and shakers of the world, and gathered into her social life members of royalty and important people from the worlds of government, business, and entertainment. She has yet to be listed in the social registers of New York and Palm Beach, but she has achieved much, much more than most of those whose names are there recorded.

NOTES

1. Estée Lauder, *Estée: A Success Story* (New York: Random House, 1985).

2. Lee Israel, *Estée Lauder: Beyond the Magic* (Englewood Cliffs, N.J.: Prentice-Hall, 1984).

3. Ibid., p. 8.

4. Lauder, *Success Story*, p. 17, 19–20.

5. Ibid., p. 24.

6. Ibid., p. 32–33.

7. Israel, *Beyond the Magic*, p. 38.

8. Lauder, *Success Story*, p. 38.

9. Israel, *Beyond the Magic*, p. 32.

10. Lauder, *Success Story*, p. 81.

11. Ibid., p. 143.

12. Israel, *Beyond the Magic*, p. 134.

13. Ibid., p. 38.

14. Lauder, *Success Story*, p. 6.

Part II

SOME
CONCLUSIONS

17

THE INTUITIVE FACTOR

Throughout the literature on the subject of intuition, reference is made to the suggestion that Einstein's theory of relativity came to him suddenly and inexplicably as he was getting onto a bus. It has been stated that much of Mozart's work came to him in dreams which he would later translate onto the keyboard. Exploring the subject of intuitive thinking, author Gail Sheehy points to the phenomenon of external and internal linkage that permits one to interrelate to nature, to others, and to the chain of existence. Says Sheehy: "It is the capacity to fantasize which makes possible leaps of imagination and invention."[1] The late Anwar Sadat, prime minister of Egypt, relied heavily on intuition to manage the affairs of his country and wrote that the best use of intuition was to avoid conflict. In Sadat's negotiations with adversaries, he knew intuitively which areas to approach with caution and which issues his adversary might be willing to negotiate.[2] An acquaintance of mine who is chief executive of a major U.S. corporation claims that effective executives tend to disassociate themselves from the detail work that follows decision making, leaving that to others. They grasp corporate problems and solutions *intuitively*!

Ralph Waldo Emerson wrote almost 150 years ago: "The primary wisdom is *intuition*. In that deep force, the last fact behind which analysis cannot go, all things find their common origin.... We lie in the lap of immense intelligence. We are the receivers of its truth and organs of its activity."[3] Available research suggests that successful entrepreneurs, both male and female, tend to exhibit a special intuitive decision-making ability. They tend to be curious and to set their personal goals in life by determining their own intuitive priorities rather than being motivated by the expectations of others. A contemporary writer on this subject found that entrepreneurs are inclined to be optimistic, seeing the glass as half-full rather than half-empty.[4] Frequently, there is evidence that they were emotionally touched in their childhood by some individual who helped them to get in touch with their ability to *feel* and thereby use intuition in making decisions.[5]

Weston Agor, the industrial psychologist, has written about intuitive decision making as a phenomenon that integrates the functions of the left side of the human brain (cognitive and analytical) with those of the right side (intuitive and creative).[6] Agor argues that right-brain skills can be cultivated and honed into a management approach to problem solving. Employing this technique, problems are solved by "first looking at the whole—often with inadequate information at hand. Decisions are then reached through intuitive insights or flashes of awareness that are received."[7] Agor cites examples of this technique in such organizations as Apple Computers, Atari, Inc., Walt Disney Enterprises, and various intelligence agencies.[8]

In *The Intuitive Manager*, author Roy Rowan makes a strong case for what he calls the "Eureka Factor," a flash of intuition which he argues is the key element in many great historical discoveries. Rowan further claims that managers of the future will learn to summon from somewhere deep inside themselves glimpses of the economic landscape ahead and intuitive flashes of the business opportunities that have yet to surface. He concludes his work with the sentence: "Hail to the future MBI—Master of Business Intuition."[9]

Agor's research on sex differences in managers' use of intuition found statistically significant differences between the sexes.[10] His and other studies suggest that women have learned to develop a keener intuitive ability necessitated historically by a need to manipulate men in positions of power in order to fulfill their own needs. Just as blind people learn to hone their other senses to a degree that enables them to "see" color through touch, women have in a similar way honed their intuitive ability to meet their needs. Other researchers have provided evidence to suggest that there may be certain physiological differences between the brains of males and females that could explain women's heightened intuitive powers.[11] For instance, scientists have been able to discern phenomenon relating to the corpus callosum, the bundle of fibers running down the center of the brain that carry impulses between the right and left hemispheres. Researchers at the Brain Research Institute at the University of California at Los Angeles have reported that the corpus callosum is a lot busier in women than in men, and that its size differs, having been found to be larger in women than in men.

Richard Pascale and Anthony Athos in *The Art of Japanese Management* have concluded that managers from an Oriental ethnic background have been conditioned from birth to focus on the Eastern world's approach to life, which is influenced by the various religions that stress the necessity of becoming mentally "in tune" with one's Creator, thus encouraging the heightened development of right-brain skills such as intuition and creativity.[12] Two of the subjects profiled in this book, Josie Natori and Maryles Casto—each born and raised in the Philippines—state that they tend to rely more heavily on intuition and "gut" feelings in making decisions than on analysis. Casto, whose roster of employees contains almost 100 percent women, even insists in the training sessions she conducts for her employees that they utilize intuitive approaches to making decisions. She ascribes her belief in this power mainly to her Eastern upbringing. Weston Agor makes reference to the manager of Mitsukoshi, Japan's largest department store, who stated that his company's success is due to the adoption of the West's pragmatic management combined with the spiritual intuitive aspects of the East.[13]

Without exception, all of the subjects interviewed for this book have pointed to the importance of intuition as a factor in entrepreneurial success. Lois Wyse cited it as one of the eight components common to successful entrepreneurial women. Lillian Katz claims that one of the four necessary ingredients in achieving entrepreneurial success lies in developing one's *instincts* and learning to trust them. She also attributes much of her own success to her creative talents stemming from the right brain.

Faith Popcorn points out that at one time in her life she worked solely on intuition, but has learned to balance it with logical analysis, hard work, determination, and self-confidence. Undoubtedly, Popcorn's keen ability to discern the future, a talent for which she enjoys a nationwide reputation, stems from her ability to extract conclusions not only from her market research, but also from that vital dimension of *visionary* intuition. Estée Lauder stated that the revelation she could build a product line to make women's faces more beautiful came to her while working with her Uncle John Schotz, when she realized that her own future was being "written in a jar of face cream," as she expressed it in her autobiography. Geraldine Stutz speaks of "knowing instinctively" in taking command of the failing fashion store, Henri Bendel's, that the store ought to be different when she conjured up an image of her famous Street of Shops which not only brought Bendel's its great success, but also provided the "boutique concept" later copied by mostly every fashion store in the world. Debrah Charatan, the youngest of all the successful subjects profiled in this book, believes that how one *feels* about things provides a frame of reference for facts "not on the surface." Charatan further attributes the females' superiority over males in this area to the fact that women are *nurturers* and take the *human* factor more seriously than men. Mary Kay Ash claims to have a keen intuitive sense that stems from her spirituality. She told me in our interview that she feels "God-directed" in her mission to demonstrate that women are equal to men in capabilities. She asserts that her intuition has enabled her instinctively to analyze the integrity of job applications in the first few minutes of an interview. She relates a significant incident. She was about to hire a man who was a real marketing whiz when she suddenly changed her mind. "I had no reason. Just intuition. Six months later, I read in the newspaper that this man had been indicted on a felony." Diane Von Furstenberg claims to do "everything" on inituition. Roy Rowan describes Diane as a visionary who chose to "run rather than cope" when she clearly saw that her clothes were losing their identity and she got out of manufacturing at the right time, switching her business into licensing.[14] When I questioned Lane Nemeth of Discovery Toys about the subject of intuition, she responded with the assertion that one uses the "right brain" sometimes without realizing it. "I'm an intuitive thinker," said Nemeth. "I believe that all previous decisions on similar problems motivate future decisions—just as though there were a computer up there accessing stored information. Thus, how one *feels* about things is the product of how the individual processes information." As to sudden flashes of intuition that produce creative ideas and concepts, Nemeth says she revels in them and speaks of them as "those great moments when you go home and know you have had an idea that made you do something ingenious. You could die for those moments—almost like taking heroin, I suppose."

Pamela Scurry focuses on her own intuitive senses in making decisions, although she doesn't overlook the essentials of logic. She sees the role of intuition as one of "opportunity finding," and cites how her logic indicated to her that her full needs required an entrepreneurial endeavor; it was her intuitive sense that enabled her to see windows of opportunities and open them when they arose. Rose Totino says: "God blessed me with a real sense of discernment. I can be with a new employee candidate for thirty minutes and by then, know whether it's going to work." This highly spiritually activated woman claims that her decision making stems from two factors: common sense and intuition in which God is her director. As she tells it: "When my big decision moments come, I look to the Lord for direction and say, 'I'll do the work, you just show me the way!' "

It would seem from my interviews with all the entrepreneurial subjects in this book that intuition without exception plays an important role in the lives of all of these successful women. Much more research needs to be done in this area, but all the evidence indicates that intuitive powers can be developed and utilized and perhaps can thereby unleash enormous personal energy and creativity.

NOTES

1. Gail Sheehy, *Passages* (New York: E. P. Dutton, 1974), p. 237.
2. Kim Wiley,, "Gut Instincts," *Savvy*, May 1986, p. 79.

3. Quoted in *Leading Edge Bulletin*, December 20, 1982.

4. Joseph R. Mancuso, *"How to Start, Finance, and Manage Your Own Small Business"* (Englewood Cliffs, N.J.: Prentice-Hall, 1984).

5. Tony Bastick, *Intuition: How We Think and Act* (New York: John Wiley & Sons, 1982).

6. Weston Agor, *Intuitive Management* (Englewood Cliffs, N.J.: Prentice-Hall, 1984).

7. Ibid., p. 1.

8. Ibid., p. 2.

9. Roy Rowan, *The Intuitive Manager* (Boston: Little, Brown & Co., 1986), p. 186.

10. Agor, *Intuitive Management*, p. 25.

11. A. E. Sargent, *The Androgynous Manager* (New York: Amacom, 1981).

12. Richard Pascale, and Anthony Athos, *The Art of Japanese Management* (New York: Warner Books, 1981).

13. Agor, *Intuitive Management*, p. 90.

14. Rowan, *The Intuitive Manager*, p. 135.

18

LOVE, MARRIAGE, AND THE ENTERPRISE

Research relating to spouses who have businesses together has been somewhat sparse, but Sharon Nelton, a journalist on the staff of *Nation's Business*, published in 1986 a commendable work, *In Love and In Business* in which she attempted to explore how entrepreneurial couples are changing the rules of business and marriage.[1] Nelton used for her research personal interviews with sixty-three individuals representing thirty-four business relationships. In nearly all cases, both spouses were interviewed together. Her project was supplemented with a questionnaire that generated responses from sixty individuals representing thirty-two businesses and thirty-three marriages. Nelton found some major actual and perceptual changes in the growing phenomenon of spouse enterprises. One significant change is expressed in the new approach to partnership—where formerly "Pop used to be the entrepreneur and Mom, the bookkeeper," Mom has now become the *entrepreneurial partner* and team player, as Nelton expressed it.[2]

Nelton cites the great entrepreneurial successes of spouses working together as she refers to well-known companies such as the Marriott Corporation, Mrs. Fields' Cookies, Häagen-Daz, and Liz Claiborne, Inc. In these enterprises, the wives are as totally involved as the husbands in a truly "his and hers" business relationship.[3]

Nelton's project offers no specific conclusions other than that there can be some major benefits when spouses successfully mesh business and personal relationships and, in so doing, find that it can *enhance* the business, the marriage, and family life. She points to examples where the sharing of problems by husband and wife in the same enterprise tends to provide a broader common ground of communication and thus a better understanding of each other. Nelton dwells at length on the case of Debbi and Randi Fields of Mrs. Fields' Cookies. The Fields have not only built a huge business in excess of $100 million in annual sales, but have generated a rewarding life-style that provides time to spend with their three children in their two homes located in Utah and Hawaii.

I could not discuss successful husband-and-wife enterprises without mentioning my friends Susie and Jim Lavenson. (Susie is national treasurer of the Committee of 200, an organization of outstanding U.S. women achievers.) Each had made unsuccessful previous marriages before they got together in late 1960s, while Jim was president of New York's Plaza Hotel. When the hotel was sold to the Westin chain, Jim was "displaced." Searching for an entrepreneurial opportunity, the Lavensons purchased the San Ysidro Ranch in Montecito, California, a badly neglected guest-ranch, overgrown with weeds but with a romantic history. Once owned by the late screen actor, Ronald Colman, it was a former hideaway retreat of celebrities such as Robert Louis Stevenson, Somerset Maugham, Winston Churchill, and John Kennedy (he and Jackie honeymooned at San Ysidro).

"For the first year, we couldn't produce a brochure because there wasn't anything we wanted to photograph," says Susie. "Also, we didn't break even until our second year—and it was no fun to lose money on a new business." By sheer determination and hard work, the Lavensons brought the ranch back to its original rustic elegance and San Ysidro again became the mecca for both celebrities and noncelebrities seeking the magic of its private ambience.

In their accomplishment, Jim gives Susie full credit for the transformation, citing her great artistic taste and the creative ingenuity she has applied to the ancient guest villas scattered about the fifty-acre property. Susie brushes off the credit for herself and points to Jim's management and marketing talents as being key to the great success of San Ysidro. The truth is, they have one of those remarkable entrepreneurial partnerships in which each plays a role that the other could not possibly play—at least as expertly. Just as Debbi and Randi Fields have provided a similar support for each other's missing talents, and in the process have nurtured their love and understanding of each other, so have the Lavensons found a deeper and more abiding mutual devotion and intimacy in their marriage.

However, not all husband-and-wife enterprises provide the bases for happy personal relationships. Some couples find that when things go wrong in business during the day, they can go wrong in the bedroom at night. Sharon Nelton's research demonstrates how a husband-and-wife enterprise, like a family business, can be more vulnerable to a personal crisis than a business where the principals are not related to each other. When couples do not readily adjust their business problems to their personal relationships, many of such marriages fail and the businesses frequently decline with the decline of the marriages. As Nelton points out: "At best, such marriages and businesses limp along while the partners carry on an uneasy truce."[4] It would appear that many such businesses which reflect a decline in spousal relationships can end in a disaster.

Consider the case of Gale and Fred Hayman, founders of the well-known Giorgio boutique in Beverly Hills, California, who developed a perfume that became an international success and occupied, until recently, the number one position of all brand-name fragrances in America. *Savvy* describes their boutique as "the world's most lavish specialty store, a virtual club for the floating principality of the very, very rich and the truly famous."[5] In 1961 Gale, then age eighteen, and Fred, then age thirty-six, were joined in wedlock. Together they purchased a small women's shop around the corner from Rodeo Drive in Beverly Hills and created a store that mirrored a club atmosphere with oak bar, billiard table, and a comfortable area for lounging. The business catered to show business personalities and other celebrities of affluence, and Giorgio's, with its familiar yellow and white awnings, became the focal point of smart shops, attracting famous up-scale names like Gucci and Van Cleef & Arpels. As their business grew, the Haymans began to drift apart emotion-ally, and in 1978 had an amicable separation but continued op-erating the business under a contract that gave each a 49 percent interest with a 2 percent interest in a fiduciary trust over which the husband had voting control.

Gale Hayman had developed, after considerable research, a fragrance launched under the name of "Giorgio." Selling for $150 an ounce, the product became *the* perfume of the people of influence in Beverly Hills. The Haymans were the first to market a fragrance using the now familiar "scent strip," an in-novative sampling technique by which a full-page advertisement releases a fragrance when the reader lifts a folded flap as di-rected.

In 1978 Robin Burns, at that time the cosmetics merchandise manager of Bloomingdale's, introduced Giorgio in Bloomie's first-floor fragrance area, thus giving the product important brand recognition. Soon other up-scale stores in the United States and abroad introduced Giorgio and sales of this fragrance skyrocketed to a staggering $100 million by 1985. "Here," said *Savvy*, "the fairytale ended suddenly. Fred banished his wife from her $2.5 million position as executive vice-president, and ousted her from all active participation in Giorgio, the store and the perfume." Gale sued Fred, demanding a multimillion dollar settlement and reinstatement as Giorgio's vice-president. Mean-while, sales of the perfume had declined, and in 1987 Giorgio was outdistanced by Obsession, the brainchild of Robin Burns who had given Giorgio its initial launch and now presides over Calvin Klein Cosmetics. The saga of the Haymans has come to a happier ending, however, with the recent purchase by Avon Corporation of the Giorgio business under an agreement whereby Fred will continue to run the Rodeo Drive store and Gale will run the fragrance business. The lawsuit between the Haymans has, of course, been withdrawn.

Arthur Lipper III, chairman and publisher of *Venture, The Mag-azine for Entrepreneurs*, gives speeches throughout the world on the many aspects of entrepreneurship, a subject that engages almost all of Lipper's incredible sixty-hour work week. In a re-cent workshop presentation where Lipper spoke before the wives of chief executives attending a major business conference, he pointed out how many successful male entrepreneurs have a lower divorce rate while building their businesses. He posed the following explanation:

The entrepreneur is excited, stimulated, frustrated, frightened, rewarded, and consumed by his business. Thus, how much emotion or energy can be left for his wife and children? How much "quality" time is there left in him after the sixteen-hour days or six- or 7-day weeks it takes to build a successful business? Extramarital involvements are not as enticing to the entrepreneur as to the nonentrepreneur, because there is so much else generating excitement in the entrepreneur's life.

Lipper continued:

That's the good news. The bad news is that, once successful, the entrepreneur tends to find himself with two things not usually available previously—money and leisure time. Very often the emotional famine experienced by the entrepreneur in his rigorous devotion to building his successful enterprise leads him to the need to reassert his manhood by indulging in the company of a younger woman, most probably *considerably* younger. Frequently, the new woman is someone with whom the entrepreneur has had, or has, a work-related relationship—someone who understands and shares the pressures and requirements of business.

Lipper's 26-year marriage to Anni—whom he refers to as his friend, advisor, and confidant, and whose office is adjacent to his—is considered a highly successful union. As he states it: "The surest way I know of for the wife and an entrepreneur to maintain their relationship is for the wife to become involved in that with which she cannot effectively *compete*, namely the business. The spouse then truly understands the operative pressures, as well as being able to savor fully the delights of success."

In a recent interview of *Venture* subscribers, it was found that 64 percent believed spouse involvement helped their marital relationship. Only 9 percent believed otherwise. In 43 percent of the cases, the wives served as members of the company's board of directors, while 39 percent served as company officers, and 35 percent served as part-time consultants.

Thus far, we have reviewed various studies of how spouse

relationships have tended to fare in entrepreneurial endeavors. While there is ample evidence to support the contention that spousal involvement in a business can enrich a marriage, the evidence is quite clear that considerably *more than half of successful entrepreneurs, both male and female, have become divorced from their mates when one of them is not involved in the enterprise.*

Of the fifteen highly successful women profiled in this book, only three have had permanently successful first marriages. All but one have been married at least once. Four have been divorced and remarried. Ten have borne children, although only seven have had more than one child. Three have been widowed and have not remarried, and nine of the fifteen have experienced the pains of divorce.

During the individual interviews I conducted with my subjects, I attempted tactfully to introduce the question of each one's marital relationship, knowing that this subject would be an important part of my research. Estée Lauder, as pointed out, was the only subject not interviewed. However, my sources among mutual friends indicated that her vital relationship with her first love, Joe Lauder, their subsequent divorce and remarriage, and her grief at his death, typifies the suggestion that the physical marriage of partners in a business relationship can only be successful when neither attempts to outdistance the other. Tensions in the Lauders' marriage began when Estée assumed the role of the more important player in providing the family income, leading to their divorce. Three years of separation from Joe convinced her, however, that the emotional needs of her life, which he supplied, meant more to her than the excitement of building her business. She returned to the marriage with the agreement that she would revert to being a team player—and apparently their marriage resumed happily.

I first met Lois Wyse in 1970, when she and her husband Marc were building a successful advertising agency with offices in Cleveland and New York. The happiness in their marriage was reflected in Lois's vibrant and captivating personality. While actively involved in the affairs of the agency, Lois managed to write sexy novels, a column in a woman's magazine, and published poems about love and marriage which clearly indicated an element of warmth and richness in her own marriage to Marc.

Her book of poems is entitled *Love Poems for the Very Married*, a clear indication of the solidarity of that marriage. However, the Wyses eventually came to a parting of the ways and each has since remarried, although they continue as business partners with Marc in charge of the Cleveland office and Lois, the New York office. When I spoke to Lois about her previous marriage, she disposed of the question with the angry response, "Look, if you are here to discuss my marital life, our interview is over!" I let the remark hang, but sensed a feeling of great bitterness and loss on her part over the break-up of her union with Marc.

As was the case with Estée and Joe Lauder, Lillian Katz's first marriage to Sam Hochberg failed when Lillian began to be the major breadwinner in the early stages of the marriage. Determined to find a way to emerge from a modest life in a small apartment, and fired with the desire to experience again the affluent life she had known as a child in Europe, Lillian started a business—like many other entrepreneurs—right out of her own home. When the business mushroomed and Lillian's attention moved in a direction much different from that of her husband, the marriage eventually fell apart and Lillian, with two sons (who are now officers of Lillian Vernon Corporation), moved on to greater things.

As in the case with most entrepreneurs, things did not go smoothly when Diane Von Furstenberg started her business. It was only her perseverance, courage, and determination to succeed that enabled her to survive the formative years when she and her titled husband Egon tackled the highly competitive New York apparel business, and eventually won. It was apparent from the beginning that Diane was the more aggressive of the two. On the other hand, Egon provided through his title of Prince a strong public relations function that would open doors otherwise closed to Diane. After two children were born during the early years of their marriage, the union went downhill fast and this glamorous couple, who had dominated the social columns of the New York press for several years, embarked upon separate lives. Diane's business continued to thrive after their separation, and it was only after ten years that the Von Furstenbergs entered into a final legal divorce. Diane claims that she and Egon remain "good friends."

Dorothy Brunson's marriage failed because she outdistanced her husband in achievements. Her incredible ambition to keep on achieving in a world quite different from that of her husband undermined their ability to communicate.

How can one attempt to explain this tendency of the first marriages of successful entrepreneurial women to fail? Let us consider the case of Debrah Charatan who had known little but hard work since she was a child. Before finishing her college education, she lived with a young lawyer eight years older than she for two years before the couple decided on a permanent, legal union. Their real estate business began as a partnership, with Debrah playing the leading role and her husband supplying the legal services through his own law practice. Debrah's long hours of work on client communication in which her husband did not participate eroded the original personal communication which had brought this couple into their marriage. It would also appear, considering the intense ambition exhibited by Debrah in her early education, that her incredible devotion to work, which she regards as part of her educational development, led her to the point where her need for a helpmate in the business became gradually less and less. Unlike the Fields and the Lavensons cited above, but more like the Lauders, the failure of the Charatan marriage appears to have stemmed from the wife's assertive role in refusing to be anything other than the dominant player on the team. It is reported that Debrah Lee Charatan even expects one day to be president of the United States.[6] One might ponder, in such a future event, whether her husband of that time would then be referred to as the "First Gentleman."

Lane Nemeth's successful record in founding Discovery Toys and pushing it to a $50 million sales enterprise in ten years had placed some strains on her relationship with Ed Nemeth, an engineer by training and her husband of some twenty-one years. The Nemeths' problems began when the pressures of the business, including both the peaks of profit success and the valleys of despair in one or two years of red figures—coupled with Lane spending most of her time on the road—took a toll on family life:

Ed and I lost communication for close to two years. However, we resolved to save our marriage. I have an exceptional husband. It's very tough to be married to him, but after twenty-one years, we've become sort of the same person. Right now, he's thinking about coming into the business—being an engineer he could be very helpful in the design and manufacture of Discovery Toys.

Jerry Stutz was married for twelve years to British artist David Gibbs. The marriage ended in 1977, but Stutz remains positive about the experience, as she tends to be about everything. "I wouldn't have missed my marriage for anything, and there were lots of terrific things about it, but it didn't endure. We seemed to grow in different directions," relates Stutz.

The forty-seven year marriage of Rose and Jim Totino, which unfortunately ended with Jim's death in 1981, was an extremely successful one. According to Rose:

Ours was a fine marriage and we were blessed with two children and nine grandchildren. One of the reasons we got along so well in our business was because Jim's real interest was in seeing that the machines in the factory were running efficiently. My Jim loved puttering with mechanical things; he could fix anything—didn't want to be bothered about business matters. That's why we got along so beautifully as a husband-and-wife team.

The marriages of two other subjects interviewed for this book appear to be eminently successful. Maryles Casto and Josie Natori, both of Philippine and Roman Catholic origin, speak of their respective mates only in glowing terms. Casto gives first priority to the needs of her husband, an outdoorsy type, and to their twelve-year-old son, taking considerable time off from her business for sailing and deep-sea diving with the two males in her life. As pointed out, Josie Natori proclaims that her marriage to Kenneth was "made in heaven," and she leans heavily on his emotional support during the many crisis periods that are characteristic of the fashion apparel industry. As her business mushroomed, Natori found it important for financially savvy Kenneth to enter her business in 1985 and provide a most helpful dimension to this growing enterprise.

To develop conclusions on this subject is difficult, indeed. There is insufficient research to provide any pattern of outcomes other than those reported above. However, what little study has been done suggests the following:

1. Entrepreneurs who become more married to their business than to their spouses tend to get divorced.
2. The presence of both spouses in the same entrepreneurial enterprise can be a great factor in nurturing the relationship. Difficulties can develop when one of the spouses trespasses on the other's turf.

NOTES

1. Sharon Nelton, *In Love and In Business* (New York: John Wiley & Sons, 1986).

2. Ibid., p. 9.

3. Ibid., p. 2.

4. Ibid., p. 25.

5. Charlene Mitchell and Thomas Burdick, "Dollars and Scents," *Savvy*, January 1987, p. 36.

6. Bruce Chadwick, "6 Women Who Made a Million or More," *Cosmopolitan*, August 1985, p. 248.

19

THE INTRAPRENEURS

Linda Wachner and Robin Burns

In recent years, Gifford Pinchot, a management consultant for well-known American corporations, coined a new word in the lexicon of business—*intrapreneurship*. In his book, *Intrapreneuring: Why You Don't Have to Leave the Corporation to Become an Entrepreneur*, Pinchot defines an intrapreneur as "any of the dreamers who *do*—those who take hands-on responsibility for creating innovation of any kind within an organization. The intrapreneur may be the creator or inventor but is always the dreamer who figures out how to turn an idea into a profitable reality."[1] Throughout this stimulating book, the author cites how major corporations, rather than allowing their innovators to slip away and start up on their own, encourage them to proceed on corporate time to develop their ideas, then assist them with the production and marketing, and further reward them with the fruits of their endeavors not only by recognition, promotion, and bonuses, but sometimes by equity enhancement through special stock options or even by establishing a subsidiary corporation to exploit the innovation and allocating to the "intrapreneur" equity participation in ownership of the subsidiary.

Some of the better-known U.S. corporations that have fostered intrapreneurship are 3M, DuPont, IBM, Texas Instruments Corporation, Hewlett-Packard, General Mills, Bank of California, and Xerox. A familiar example of the intrapreneurial process is the case of Art Fry of 3M Corporation, who invented Post-it

Notes, the little yellow pads with a band of adhesive substance at the top of the back side which are now used throughout the world for handwritten messages. Taking advantage of a 3M policy that gives technical people 15 percent of their time to work on innovative ideas of their own, the persistent Fry found ways of drawing on all the technical, production, research, and marketing resources of 3M. All these efforts produced a $300 million one-product annual sales figure, and as Pinchot points out, "Art Fry now is recognized by his company as a member of the Carlton Society—3M's Innovation Hall of Fame."[2] It is indicated that Fry's personal new worth was considerably enhanced as a result of his intrapreneurial efforts.

Another technique for rewarding the entrepreneurial spirit of senior corporate managers is through the process of the "leveraged buyout." This process permits senior management to acquire total or, at least, effective control of an enterprise through the purchase of existing corporate stock of the company by an investment banking concern which then underwrites bonds to finance the acquisition of the equity shares of the enterprise. These bonds are known by the familiar phrase "junk bonds," made popular by the operations of Wall Street organizations such as Drexel, Burnham & Company, Morgan Stanley, and others.

The leveraged buyout process provides senior management, employing comparatively little risk capital of their own, to acquire a "leveraged" opportunity that promises to provide a large capital gain in the future, *provided* the company prospers sufficiently to service the large debt it acquires in the process. This technique is often used when publicly owned corporations "go private." An example of the process is Warnaco, an old-line apparel firm headquartered in Bridgeport, Connecticut. Warnaco's stock traded on the New York Stock Exchange until it went private in 1985 under the guidance of Linda Wachner, a superachieving entrepreneurial woman who, with the financial support of Drexel, gained effective control of the apparel company whose roster of brand names include Warner brassieres, Pringle Sweaters, Hathaway Shirts, and White Stag Sportswear. Annual sales in 1986 totaled $600 million. Wachner expects to make Warnaco the largest apparel company in the world, and if her goals for the company are met, she will build for herself a huge personal fortune.

Wachner's business background includes a stint at Associated Merchandising Corporation, a New York buying office that represents major U.S. department stores. One of these, Foley's of Houston, Texas, transferred her to Texas to buy apparel. When she returned later to New York at the age of twenty-two, Macy's hired her as their bra and girdle buyer. Wachner saw an opportunity of boosting the sales of bras by taking them out of the discreet boxes in which they had always been packaged, and putting them on hangers. This innovative technique is now copied by every major retailer in America.

Wachner's success at Macy's was soon observed by Warnaco, whose Warner division (bras, girdles, and foundation garments) needed someone to beef up sales. After a seven-year association during which she was a senior vice-president, she was hired away by Max Factor, one of the world's largest cosmetics manufacturers, which was having profitability problems. During her five-year tenure at Max Factor, she was able to convert $16 million of losses into a $5 million operating profit. All this was accomplished in two years during which time she got rid of much of the company's extravagance and waste. Promoted over the heads of many men, tensions grew and Wachner resigned in 1984 to join a venture capital firm whose then objective was to acquire control of Revlon, the huge cosmetics firm. A fierce bidding match ensued; Wachner and her associates were outbid for the acquisition of Revlon and the persistent Wachner began stalking elsewhere. Targeting Warnaco, her old alma mater, as a logical objective to satisfy her thirst to run a big company in a field she knows well, Wachner teamed up with Spectrum Group in California, and with the junk bond financing by Drexel, Burnham and Company, successfully purchased Warnaco from its existing stockholders for $46.50 per share thus bringing the company private.

Born in New York in 1947, the daughter of a fur salesman, Linda Wachner was always regarded as a "smart kid." Plagued with a chronic spine ailment, she spent the eleventh year of her life in a body brace from head to knees, almost completely immobilized. She graduated from high school at age sixteen and entered Buffalo University where her extracurricular activities focused on administrative jobs. She proctored exams, graded papers, and worked in the dean's office. Over Christmas vacations, she came home to work at New York's old Best & Company, where she got hooked on retailing. During her earlier years at Warnaco, Wachner, then twenty-five, married a man thirty years her senior who died in 1983. She has remained a widow.

The above information concerning Linda Wachner is a distillation of various articles concerning her remarkable accomplishments that have appeared in *Fortune* and *Business Week*. A lengthy article about her was published in the *New York Times* business section on April 22, 1987. Describing her as "one of the highest ranking businesswomen in America," the article reported that Wachner developed as a teenager a fierce longing for around-the-clock activity after spending much of childhood in a body brace. "Her present life as a widow is crammed with skiing, golfing and tennis dates, partly to make up for those years of confinement. Throw in her positions on several prominent boards and it becomes apparent that Wachner, an admitted workaholic, does much of her sleeping while airborne," the article relates. Last year, Wachner earned close to $1 million, including incentive pay. Drexel Burnham Lambert hopes to take Warnaco public again if all goes well, in which case Linda Wachner could come out with an intrapreneurial reward of $50 million.

One of the fastest growing marketing companies in America and certainly one whose stock value has commanded the attention of private and institutional investors alike is Minnetonka, Inc., a Minnesota enterprise founded with a $3,000 initial investment by entrepreneur Robert Taylor, who began selling soapballs he made in his basement in the late 1960s. Annual sales of this company now exceed $200 million. The company's product mix include shampoos, liquid soaps, home and personal fragrances, and hair treatments. In 1978 Minnetonka acquired Calvin Klein Cosmetics Company from Calvin Klein, the well-known fashion designer, hoping to develop a large business in cosmetics around the publicity surrounding Klein's position as one of America's most important names in women's fashions.

Sales and profits of Minnetonka's acquisition floundered until the frustrated Taylor, in 1983, persuaded Robin Burns, then cosmetics merchandise manager at Bloomingdale's, to leave her job and become president of the Calvin Klein Cosmetics subsidiary of Minnetonka, Inc.

From the moment Burns took over the subsidiary company, this intrapreneurial young woman made things happen. Just nine years out of college, the thirty-year-old Burns capitalized on her Bloomingdale's training, and relying on her keen intuitive characteristics, began effecting dramatic changes in the company. Burns phased out the cosmetics segment of the product line in 1985, as she focused on introducing a new woman's fragrance, Obsession, followed in 1986 with Obsession for Men, and utilizing dramatic new advertising and distribution techniques, made it the number-one-selling fragrance in America. This transformation converted a sizeable string of losses in Minnetonka's Calvin Klein subsidiary to an operating profit that now contributes approximately one-half of the corporation's total profits. It has also pushed the market value of Minnetonka stock from $3.50 per share in 1984 to $30 per share in early 1987. (The stock was split 2 for 1 in May of 1987).[3]

Robin Burns occupies a unique position on the Minnetonka corporate officer team in that the Calvin Klein subsidiary she presides over is headquartered in New York, with a factory in New Jersey, while all other Minnetonka divisions function out of its Minnesota facility. Burns not only receives a handsome salary and bonus, but can and will receive shares of the parent company worth several millions of dollars, provided certain minimum goals are achieved in her domain.

Burns had spent nine years with Bloomingdale's and had no experience running a production company before coming to Minnetonka. However, she operates on the principle that a person can learn almost anything by asking questions and listening closely. She sees herself as very much the "people" person she has proven to be, and has surrounded herself with a highly talented roster of personnel in all management positions. Calvin Klein's own corporation receives a percentage royalty of the sales of this subsidiary of Minnetonka. Burns and Klein together designed the ingredients and packaging of Obsession, and drawing on Burns's retail experience at Bloomingdale's, developed a marketing strategy requiring a promotional expenditure in excess of $10 million to launch the product. Using highly sensual and provocative TV commercials and magazine ads, the launch of Obsession (at $160 an ounce) was an extraordinary success. The controversial advertising was an extra boost for sales because it was freely discussed on all three morning TV network shows and in countless newspaper and magazine articles. The Sunday evening TV program *Sixty Minutes* devoted twenty minutes of prime time to the controversy, driving even more people into stores to buy the product. The subsidiary's sales soared to $30 million in the first nine months after the launch and a new career for intrapreneur Robin Burns was fully in place.

Burns's background closely follows that of many of the entrepreneurial women profiled in this book. The only child of divorced parents, Robin Burns has a healthy relationship with her mother. Burns was motivated by her mother's entrepreneurial drive. Although Burns lived in a small, upper-class community of Colorado Springs, financial circumstances did not permit Robin the life of affluence enjoyed by other neighborhood children. That, however, did not deter her from achieving success socially, academically, and athletically. "At school, I was always active in extracurricular activities and I loved to participate competitively in all outdoor sports such as skating and skiing," recalls Burns, who was also an honor student.

Her great desire as a teenager to experience life outside of Colorado prompted Burns's application for a scholarship to Syracuse University, which she received. That scholarship, which was supplemented with money earned by cocktail waitressing nights and weekends, allowed her the opportunity to participate in a varied roster of extracurricular activities. "My experience on Syracuse's campus was an education in living and, of course, demanding academic subjects", relates Burns, who majored in business. She joined a sorority in 1971.

Burns recalls her decision to join Kappa Kappa Gamma. "The house offered better food, housing, and style of living than that of the old prewar dormitory I had been assigned to." Her leadership abilities were emerging even then. "They made me rush chairman in my sophomore year. I accepted their offer and ques-

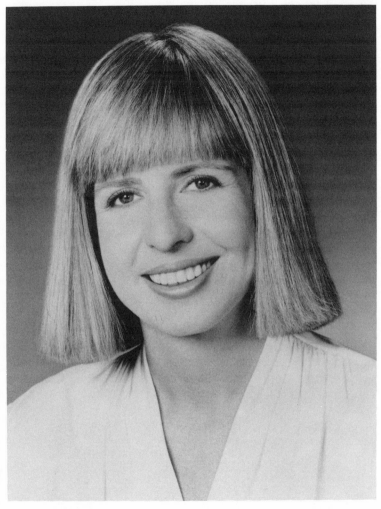

Photo by Bob Kiss   Robin Burns

tioned the superficiality of rush programs on campus. The silver tea services and dresses for dinner were so different from the reality of life, so I decided to change all this. My peers said I couldn't do it, but I saw the value of promoting reality. I prevailed and we got the biggest pledge class of anyone that year," she relates. Following this accomplishment, Burns was elected president of her sorority the following year.

When campus recruiters from Bloomingdale's visited Syracuse, Burns was selected to enter their executive training program as soon as she graduated. "I had a feeling that going to New York City would be the training ground for me to find out what I really wanted. This was, in my plans, to be a six-month trial period. Never did I think I would stay at Bloomies beyond that time," she recalls. "I was there nine years until I left to join Minnetonka. Every time I was ready to leave, I got promoted and eventually became merchandise manager of cosmetics."

Burns cites Bloomingdale's as a retail environment full of challenge. It is a tough training ground where one learns to develop products, to negotiate, to deal with people, including management as well as subordinates. All of these elements contribute to building a successful business. Consistency and determination to complete tasks are also key to success. "Bloomingdale's is such a competitive environment and the pace is so stimulating, it requires a lot of energy and so, unless you move forward, you fail and drop out. Out of the twenty-eight in my training class, there were only two or three of us left after three years," recalls Burns.

Being an effective decision maker is also key to entrepreneurial success, says Burns. "One must learn early on to effectively evaluate a situation, review all possible options, the up side and the down side, and to make a decision. This process must be achieved with economy of time. Your worst decision is to not make a decision or to procrastinate. Timing is often critical. It is crucial, also, to include senior executives as partners in the decision-making process. Leadership continues to be one of my strongest roles at Calvin Klein."

Robin Burns, at age thirty-five and single, continues to strive for balance between her career and personal life. "I achieve that essential balance by taking care of my health and that includes regular workouts. And I leave time for fun activities which include fishing and skiing with friends. I also build leisure time into my hectic schedule."

Intrapreneurs like Robin Burns and Linda Wachner bear the same entrepreneurial characteristics of those women who preside over businesses they created. They demonstrate the same self-confidence, courage, creativity, intuitiveness, and energy level to be found in other women of their ilk. They symbolize the modern trend among corporations to make an entrepreneurial system work inside the organization. As Gifford Pinchot sums up his research efforts: "Intrapreneurship is not just a way to increase the level of innovation and productivity of organizations, although it is doing that. More importantly, it is a way of organizing businesses so that work again becomes a joyful expression of one's contribution to society."[4]

NOTES

1. Pinchot, Gifford, *Intrapreneuring*, 1985, New York, N.Y., Harper & Row.

2. Ibid., p. 284.

3. The history of Minnetonka indicates that its founder and chief executive officer, Robert Taylor, knows how to select and motivate associates who share the entrepreneurial spirit that prompted Taylor to leave Johnson & Johnson in the mid-sixties and found Minnetonka, Inc. The company's employee stock-option plan and corporate performance share awards under Taylor's leadership have been key factors in the dramatic growth of this highly innovative company. One thousand dollars invested in Minnetonka stock in 1970 would have a market value in 1988 of approximately $100,000.

4. Pinchot, *Intrapreneuring*, p. 284.

20

STRATEGIES FOR SUCCESS— FIVE PRINCIPLES

One can find numerous "how-to" books on entrepreneurship and the management of small businesses. Some 300 American colleges and universities currently offer courses on the subject. The how-to books and the various texts and course syllabi trace a standard pattern of steps to follow in the start-up phase of a new enterprise. In consequence, a kind of discipline or organized body of knowledge seems to be developing within the practice of entrepreneurship.

We academics who teach courses in management remind our students that the process of managing an enterprise is *both* a science and an art. It is a science in that certain basic principles have developed over the years that have withstood the tests and challenges of time. Those principles, we claim, should be observed by managers because they provide useful guides in shaping plans that are designed to achieve defined goals. Such plans are labeled *strategies*. We tell our students that management is also an art in that the technical, human, and conceptual skills of management can be learned only through experience. So it also appears to be with the practice of entrepreneurship, where we emphasize the practical aspects of developing formal business plans, making cash flow projections, creating the initial form of organization (sole proprietorship, partnership, or corporation), finding sources of investment funds, dealing with lawyers, banks, advertising agencies, accountants, and suppliers, and finally "growing" the business to the point where its founder, or founders, can reap the riches of capital gains through the process of going public or by being acquired by another company.

A recent publication authored by Roger Fritz, "*Nobody Gets Rich by Working for Someone Else—An Entrepreneur's Guide*," stresses all of the above as being essential in starting or purchasing a new business.[1] He and other authors on the subject cite real-life cases involving strategies that successful entrepreneurs have used in the process of starting and building their businesses. Does an analysis of these successful strategies provide the basis for developing certain principles that can make the study of entrepreneurship more of a science and less of an art? We appear to be moving in that direction. But much more work and study needs to be done.

The publications of Hisrich, Brush, and Scollard (mentioned in chapter 1) have attempted to concentrate on the subject of entrepreneurial women. Their tasks, as well as mine, have the purpose of trying to narrow the gap in the literature concerning women entrepreneurs. One objective of my inquiry was to identify some of the most important strategies for success that my sample group could cite from their own experiences.

Let us then examine the cases of my subjects and attempt to distill from their records some of the strategies—common to all—that they found important in starting, organizing, and growing their enterprises. From this exercise, five principles emerge that can serve as guides for formulating successful entrepreneurial strategies:

1. *Successful Entrepreneurs Obtain Experience at an Early Age.*
When and how does the early spark of entrepreneurship begin to glow? As children, many of us were given household chores to perform, for which our parents contributed small amounts of money to teach us that work had its monetary rewards. Some of us advanced into jobs outside the home, taking on paper routes, baby-sitting, or setting up those time-honored curbside lemonade stands on hot summer days. Many writers suggest that here is where the seeds of the entrepreneurial spirit are planted; here is where the need for achievement in the market-

place is fostered. Here is where the drama of becoming rich begins.

An examination of the early life history of most well-known business founders indicates that each had some business experience during the days of their youth. The subjects profiled in this book are no exception. Lillian Katz worked after school in a candy store; Faith Popcorn clerked in her grandfather's haberdashery; Debrah Charatan arose at 4 A.M. each morning to work in a bakery; Pamela Scurry as a young teenager made and sold jewelry; Estée Lauder worked in a department store across the street from her childhood home; Lois Wyse worked as a newspaper reporter when she was a teenager; and Robin Burns spent her high school summers working in a bank.

2. *Successful Entrepreneurs Seek Out and Find "Niche" Opportunities.*

Entrepreneurship is market-focused. Entrepreneurs perceive a customer need for the product or service which initiates the idea to start a business. For example, Estée Lauder saw a customer need for the face creams her Uncle John taught her to make while she attended high school. As she states it, "My reputation among my peers at Newtown High School grew by leaps and bounds. I gave away gallons of cream to my friends."[2] Later, she carved out a niche for her line of beauty products, as she traveled to resort areas giving free facials to customers in beauty salons. Mary Kay Ash discovered that a face-cream formula that was originally used in the tanning of animal hides would do wonderful things for the human skin. Then, opportunist Mary Kay proceeded to sell $200,000 worth of her products derived from this formula in her first year, followed by $800,000 of sales in her second year. Her previous experience in direct marketing with Stanley Home Products triggered her decision to distribute Mary Kay Cosmetics through home demonstrations, and she eventually built a business in excess of $300 million in annual sales! Stockbroker Muriel Siebert found herself in competition with the major giant firms of Wall Street. She saw only opportunity when a change in the law permitted her to grab a special niche in brokering large blocks of stocks at discounted rates. Lane Nemeth saw a great void in the character of children's toys and found her niche in producing and selling toys that were educationally oriented. Diane Von Furstenberg combined her acquired knowledge of silky-jersey fabric with her talent for self-promotion in creating the little wrap dress, a stunning success at a time when the women's fashion industry was thirsty for a new look in dresses. Her creations with the "Princess Diane Von Furstenberg" label quickly identified her as a priestess of fashion and carved out an accepted niche for her in that market. When Geraldine Stutz took over the aging, money-losing Henri Bendel's, she saw an opportunity and restructured the store into a place that catered to a defined segment of the fashion market—sophisticated, small-size women who loved clothes. Her unique Street of Shops was a great hit and thereby created a special niche for Bendel's among New York's top fashion stores. As a flight attendant, the canny and ambitious Maryles Casto learned a great deal about the needs and wants of business travellers. Starting her own travel agency, she capitalized on the opportunities emanating from all she had learned as a flight attendant by offering services through her agency that went far beyond those of her competitors. And when Josie Natori saw a niche opportunity in quality lingerie with her unique embroidery styling, she took advantage of her Philippines connections and captured an untapped market in America.

3. *Successful Entrepreneurs Build Strong Teams of Associates.*
Entrepreneurs who start and preside over successful enterprises are usually talented, ambitious, and hard-working individuals who demand much of themselves. They tend to set high standards of excellence and find it difficult to tolerate mediocrity in others. In consequence, they surround themselves with associates from whom they expect the same characteristics they see in themselves, and in the process strive to build winning teams. Dorothy Brunson, for example, puts in long hours at her job and expects the same from her associates. She stated in my interview with her: "Rather than pay each of two ordinary people a $25,000 salary, I would rather find one person who will work as I do and pay that person $50,000." The worldwide growth of Estée Lauder Cosmetics is unquestionably attributable to the founder's ability to surround herself with a strong team of key players. Her son Leonard was groomed as a youth to

eventually preside capably over his family's billion-dollar enterprise which Estée Lauder initiated almost a half-century ago. Successful entrepreneurs are usually quick to spot their own deficiencies in important skills and knowledge, and recruit for their enterprises others who can provide what the founders are lacking. This is particularly true in matters of accounting and finance. Rose Totino's frozen pizza enterprise could not have flourished in the manner it did had she not recruited an executive team to cover all the areas in which she was lacking expertise. Looking back on her successful business life, the modest Rose told me: "I had no managerial experience, but knew how to make a good pizza, when there was no competition in pizzas. Had I understood then all of the ramifications of building a business, I might not have started in the first place. Thank the Lord for the wonderful people who helped me!"

4. *Successful Entrepreneurs Make Friends with Their Bankers and Suppliers.*

All of the recent how-to publications on entrepreneurship point to the wisdom of developing good relations with a local bank. One often reads these words of advice: "Know your *banker* not your bank." In the start-up days of my own business, I found a great truth in the advertising slogan: "You Have a Friend at Chase Manhattan." Chase's bank officer assigned to the account of Russel Taylor, Inc. became well acquainted with me during the time I had presided over the company from which I resigned to start out on my own. In consequence, that relationship was not only a great source of wise advice, it generated a confidence that permitted my company to obtain a much-needed line of credit that was far beyond the actual original dollar equity of my business. Those who have written about entrepreneurial ventures started by women point to the problems they often experience in obtaining bank credits. Bankers tend to view women's applications for loans and credit lines with skeptical eyes, particularly those who have had no financial backgrounds. Commenting on this point, Lillian Vernon Katz recommends: "When you talk to a banker about money, never dress in casual clothes. Be honest about your business plan. Many women tend to oversell themselves, when it's clear they haven't got all the details worked out. Before you meet your banker, make sure you're well prepared to discuss all of your financial matters." No woman entrepreneur knows this better than Lane Nemeth whose firm, Discovery Toys, nearly went bankrupt three times as funds ran out. When one of these crises arose in 1981, the persuasive Nemeth told me she literally sat in a local banker's office and refused to leave until she had persuaded the banker to provide a much-needed $250,000 loan! When Rose Totino tried to borrow $1,500 from a local bank to start her little pizza shop, the loan officer told her he had never heard of pizzas. Rose came back the next day with pizzas she had baked for him, and he was so impressed with this unique product that the bank purchased a full-page newspaper ad to launch the opening of Totino's Pizza Kitchen.

Just as one should develop a strong banking connection in a start-up business, it follows that a good relationship with all suppliers of materials and services is of equal importance. New businesses frequently find themselves short of sufficient working capital. Many run short of cash by paying their bills at the normal due dates. Because suppliers tend to view a start-up customer as an opportunity, they will often permit "extra dating" or delayed payment of thirty to sixty days to help that new customer. This help is not given automatically—it must be asked for. Estée Lauder, for example, launched Youth Dew at a time when her company's liquidity for paying bills was running tight. According to Lee Israel's account of the perfume's successful launch, the fragrance was developed by International Flavors and Fragrances (IFF) as a favor to Estée by its president, her old friend A. L. van Amerigen. The book relates that "van Amerigen's company really backed her heavily when she didn't have enough money to buy materials. They gave her credit when she needed it badly."[3] Eventually, the assistance paid off for IFF when Estée's company later became this supplier's most loyal and important customer—as it is to this day.

Lillian Katz highly recommends that entrepreneurs should make friends with their suppliers. As she told me: "Sometimes they are willing to hold on to your supplies until you actually need them. This keeps the goods in their inventory, not yours—and that helps your cash flow. Also when you need goods in a hurry to supply immediate orders, a friendly supplier will make the extra effort to take care of your needs."

5. *Successful Entrepreneurs Learn to Understand Financial Statements.*

Accounting is the language of business. Without some accounting literacy, anyone starting a new enterprise is asking for trouble. Most small business failures are preceeded by a dearth of cash, and it is for this reason that all college and university courses in entrepreneurship stress budgeting and cash flow projections as a major segment of those courses.

Among the subjects interviewed for this book, those who had some previous accounting knowledge emphasized the great value of it. Josie Natori believes she could never have survived in her new lingerie venture had she not taken business courses at college, and especiallly courses in accounting. Those who had a professional background in accounting—Muriel Siebert and Dorothy Brunson, for example—found the start-up processes of their enterprises much easier as a result of their financial knowledge. Estée Lauder's husband Joe, who was a trained accountant, made the task of growing the business less complicated for Estée whose great talents and skills lay in the marketing area. Mary Kay Ash rejoices in her good fortune of having her trusted son Roger trained in the area of finance, so that she can devote her talents elsewhere. When Jerry Stutz acquired Bendel's, and with no accounting background, she admits to having been intimidated, even "terrified" by financial matters. Nevertheless, realizing how important it was to digest the store's financial reports with a full understanding, the determined Stutz made up her mind to learn about such matters, and learn she did. Lillian Katz and Lane Nemeth each admit that the major financial crises each experienced stemmed from their insufficient knowledge of accounting and financial matters. From this emerges a derivative principle: *If you don't understand accounting, hire a capable accountant and begin to learn it yourself.*

As stated above, principles must withstand the tests and challenges of time. Some people tend to think that observing principles restricts creative effort rather than guiding it and making it richer and more profitable. Some entrepreneurs with great creative talent also stumble and fall, and the sad record shows that more than half of new business starts in America do not make it through their first four years. New business founders can follow the important steps outlined in the how-to books, but unless they also observe the fundamental principles outlined above, the life expectancies of their enterprises are likely to be short.

NOTES

1. Roger Fritz, *Nobody Gets Rich by Working for Someone Else—An Entrepreneur's Guide* (New York: Dodd, Mead & Co., 1987).

2. Estée Lauder, *Estée: A Success Story* (New York: Random House, 1985), p. 20.

3. Lee Israel, *Estée Lauder: Beyond the Magic* (Englewood Cliffs, N.J.: Prentice-Hall, 1984), p. 41.

21

THE NATURE OF THE ENTREPRENEURIAL WOMAN

In chapter 1, reference was made to Hisrich and Brush's studies in which the authors attempted to draw a common profile of characteristics they found in their research sample of 468 women entrepreneurs.[1] Among their findings was a refutation of the common opinion that women are strongly dependent and passive and that, in fact, the typical woman entrepreneur resembles her male counterpart in most personality areas.[2] The following table indicates a self-assessment of the personality characteristics from the respondents of their sample. The right-hand column lists those personality characteristics typically attributed to male entrepreneurs. The left column lists diametrically opposite characteristics.

Although a number of the other characteristics emerging from my much smaller sample do confirm some of Hisrich and Brush's findings, some do not. They found, for instance, that the majority are first-born children from a middle- or upper-class family in which the father was self-employed. No pattern to confirm this emerged from my sample.

Hisrich and Brush reported that "nearly 70 percent of all women entrepreneurs have a college education, many with graduate degrees; their parents, particularly their fathers, and their spouses are also well educated."[3] Half of my subject entrepreneurs have only high school diplomas or did not complete

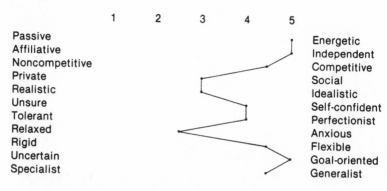

Personality Characteristics of Women Entrepreneurs.

SOURCE: The Woman Entrepreneur
          Characteristics of Women Entrepreneurs.
          Hisrich & Brush: Lexington Books, p. 27 (Reproduced with permission of the authors)

college, and, with a few exceptions, their parents were not highly educated.

Hisrich and Brush found that the strongest motivators for women starting their own businesses were needs for independence, job satisfaction, and achievement. As they stated it, "Women entrepreneurs tend to be more interested in self-fulfillment than in money and power."[4] My smaller sample of superachieving women tends to confirm this.

It would appear that there is a need for much more research that addresses the subject of the psyche of entrepreneurial women. The commonalities among all entrepreneurial people, regardless of gender, appear to flow in distinct patterns. Accordingly, the following characteristics and influences are suggested as fruitful areas for further expansion and study. Let us then summarize this work by analyzing each as applied to the individuals profiled herein.

- Creativity and ability to innovate
- Self-confidence
- Drive for autonomy

- Courage
- Education
- Energy level
- Intuition (see chapter 17)
- Luck and other environmental influences

CREATIVITY AND ABILITY TO INNOVATE

The literature concerning entrepreneurship seems to stress that a true entrepreneur is seen as an innovator. In the early 1950s, Harvard economist Joseph Schumpeter stated: "The function of entrepreneurs is to reform or evolutionize the pattern of production by exploiting an invention or, more generally, an untried technological possibility for a new commodity or producing an old one in a new way, opening a new source of supply of materials or a new outlet for products, by reorganizing a new industry."[5]

Hisrich and Brush give the following definition of entrepreneurial behaviors: "Entrepreneurship is the process of creating something different of value by devoting the necessary time and effort, by the accompanying financial, psychological, and social risks, and by receiving the resulting rewards of monetary and personal satisfaction."[6]

It would appear fair to state that not every new business is entrepreneurial. While, for instance, an entrepreneurial type person may open another restaurant in an American suburb, the process is not really entrepreneurial because the founder is merely attempting to capture a share of an existing market. He or she gambles on the increasing popularity of eating out, but does not really create a new satisfaction or a new consumer demand. Peter Drucker uses the example of McDonald's to illustrate this perspective. Ray Kroc, the founder of McDonald's, did not invent the hamburger, but applied new processes and tools, new training concerning analysis of work to be done, and set new standards to upgrade the yield from existing resources, thereby creating a *new market* and a *new customer*. Thus, claims Drucker, Kroc was indeed an entrepreneur.[7]

Estée Lauder innovated an approach to helping women enhance their beauty through her creation of facial creams and new marketing techniques that placed her products in dominant positions on the main floors of every major department store in the world. Mary Kay Ash exploited and expanded a direct-selling technique by which her trained demonstrators present her beauty products directly to consumers in their own homes. This same technique inspired a frustrated Lane Nemeth to utilize a similar marketing channel to deliver educational toys to parents wishing to buy toys other than teddy bears and laser guns for their children. Nemeth saw a market niche that needed filling, and used an existing technique to fill it—at the rate of $50 million in annual sales, and still growing. When New York State laws covering transactions between stockbrokers and clients were modified to permit negotiable rather than fixed rates, Muriel Siebert saw a window of opportunity and built an innovative brokerage business that trades large blocks of securities at commissions far below those of the prominent, traditional, brokerage houses—and, in the process, created a new market and new customers for herself.

Theodore Levitt, the well-known marketing pundit and currently editor of the *Harvard Business Review*, notes that "entrepreneurs have the ability to see opportunities before they become."[8] The ability to sniff out opportunity appears to have been a talent of all great innovators throughout history. It is seen in the successes of Thomas Edison, Henry Ford, Alexander Graham Bell, Thomas Watson, Sears and Roebuck, George Eastman, Henry Luce, Walt Disney—and each of the subjects of this book. Most of these entrepreneurs did not create things that had not been done before, because in most cases someone else had previously invented the product or process that has become associated with their names. For instance, Eastman did not invent the camera—as many people believe—but replaced the heavy glass plates used in photography in the mid–1880s with a cellulose film and then designed a lightweight box camera around his film. Eastman Kodak took world leadership in photography and still retains it. Henry Ford did not invent the automobile; he designed a car that could be totally mass-produced, largely by semiskilled labor on an assembly line, and marketed at a price affordable to people with moderate incomes—a segment of the population that Ford could see as an inviting market segment for the sale of cars. Ford created a new customer.

While none of the superachieving women who are the principal subjects of this book invented new products or processes, they all are creative innovators. They have not sat on their haunches, waiting for things to happen or someone else to do it—*they made things happen* themselves. They all demonstrate that creativity and innovation are the specific tools of the entrepreneur—the means by which *change* is utilized to create a different business or service, and a new customer.

SELF-CONFIDENCE

At an early age, Debrah Lee Charatan, the youngest entrepreneur profiled in this book, began to resent authority. Her outstanding drive for autonomy was fueled by the anger she felt when she was displaced in her real estate job by a male. With a self-confidence that was untarnished by this event, Charatan opened her own business and began an upward climb that will be satisfied probably only when she occupies the Oval Office of the White House. Successful beyond description in her six-year-old business that grosses over $200 million a year, this thirty-one-year-old millionairess epitomizes that characteristic of self-confidence to be found in all successful women entrepreneurs and intrapreneurs.

The characteristic of self-confidence tends to dispel the myth that entrepreneurs are great risk takers. On the contrary, successful entrepreneurs tend to be *risk avoiders*. They see a situation from an entirely different angle. As mentioned above, they perceive the need for a product, a service, a market, or a niche in an existing market not seen or anticipated by others. When Faith Popcorn, for instance, developed the conviction that most advertising agencies were not sufficiently in touch with customers to properly advise clients about marketing strategies, she developed a methodology that provides an honest resource for consumer attitudes. She *knew* her methodology could not fail, for the need was obvious in her perception. Entrepreneurial people often see their abilities and capacities as essentially unlimited, because they are *confident*, not arrogant or reckless. The word "failure" seldom enters their vocabulary, unless someone else brings it in. For instance, when Geraldine Stutz was converting Bendel's from a disaster into a robust business, and in the process had to face the obstacles that even her associates considered dangerous risks, the thought of failure never occurred to Stutz. As she pointed out, "We had lots of crises, and many dark days, but I knew I was on the right track in steering the enterprise toward our basic goal."

John Hines, president of Continental Illinois Venture Corporation which deals with the financing of enterpreneurial start-ups, describes this quality of entrepreneurial self-confidence as "the tenacity which separates the doer from the quitter. Tenacity is also very difficult to judge and is often confused with stubbornness or inflexibility," claims Hines.[9] The quality of self-confidence does not shine forth as arrogance, stubbornness, or even bravado. It appears to reflect more the internal skills of self-mastery or the ability to develop and capitalize on one's known capabilities. Psychologist Charles Garfield claims that self-confidence stems from the feeling—and the evidence to back it up—that you know what you are doing, and do it well.[10]

Self-confidence is a characteristic that is certainly common to all of the subjects interviewed for this book. All exhibit a sense of expertise in their own fields and the knowledge that if something goes wrong they will know how to deal with it. In short, all seem to trust their own effectiveness. "To be successful as a woman, you have to be better than a man," said Pamela Scurry when I interviewed her. According to Mae Yue, Minnesota's venture capitalist, "women have to be three to five times better than men to succeed."[11] That kind of self-confidence is seen in each of the subjects of this book.

DRIVE FOR AUTONOMY

The drive for autonomy seems to be a common characteristic of all successful entrepreneurs, particularly women. A feature story in *Business Week*, which referred back eleven years to a previous cover story on the top 100 corporate women it had reviewed in 1976, reported that many of them have now become frustrated at their slow progress up the corporate ladder. The article relates: "Many are sticking it out, resigned to the idea that they may advance—but never to the highest corporate offices. Others have abandoned big companies to start their own businesses, new careers, or families."[12] This tends to confirm the continuing existence of male-imposed barriers to women in the corporate world as best explained by Lois Wyse, profiled in chapter 2, who stated that "America will see a woman in the White House before we will see a woman CEO of General Motors."

The frustrations of seven of the subjects of this book drove them out of existing corporate jobs when they confronted the barriers on the upper rungs of the corporate ladder and decided to strike out on their own. One of them, Mary Kay Ash, sincerely believes that her entire career has been directed by the Almighty with the definite mission to demonstrate that women can be equally effective as men, not by trying to act like "one of the boys" but by maintaining their individual femininity.

EDUCATION

There does not appear to be any correlation between entrepreneurial success and a high level of formal education. Half of the subjects profiled in this study have only high school diplomas, and of these, only three had more than two years of college. Seven of the fifteen have bachelor's degrees, and only two of those seven have obtained master's degrees—and not one has earned an MBA. The two corporate intrapreneurs profiled in chapter 9 have bachelor's degrees. At least four have been awarded honorary doctorates by several colleges or universities for their outstanding achievements.

As a teacher of business subjects, with a commitment to education, I made it a point to discuss the matter of business and economics literacy with all of the women interviewed. Among those whose educational background was in the liberal arts, all with two exceptions felt they were deficient in such subjects as accounting, finance, and computer science. They either had to teach themselves during the course of their careers or find trusted associates from whom those responsibilities could be exacted. Mary Kay Ash to this day is bored with all the financial aspects of her business, leaving such matters almost entirely to her son, Richard Rogers. Lillian Katz's firm, with annual sales of $125 million, ran into serious difficulties in 1984 because of Katz's own lack of knowledge concerning budgets and inventory controls. Reflecting on this, Katz said in my interview with her, "I should have taken one of those Harvard courses." In the early years of her business, Estée Lauder leaned heavily on her accounting-trained husband for all matters of finance, and later sent her two sons to graduate business schools to they could fill this important function of their growing enterprise. Geraldine Stutz, a product of a pure liberal arts education, admits she didn't know what she was doing when she had to assume the added burden of financial responsibility after buying Henry Bendel's. "So I learned—because I simply had to," said Stutz. Rose Totino, whose formal education ceased at the tenth grade, can add and multiply figures in her head with remarkable speed and accuracy, but is completely lacking in the most simple areas of business skills except for those skills having to do with people. Her incredibly keen intuitive sense in selecting and motivating capable people for the team of managers she needed in order to build her multimillion dollar pizza business is a dramatic illustration of the fact that formal education does not necessarily correlate with success in starting and building an enterprise.

Josie Natori points to her educational background as an economics major at Manhattanville College and said to me during our interview, "Fortunately I also took courses in accounting while I was in college—otherwise, I don't think I would ever have had the confidence to start my own business." Muriel Siebert also considers the economics and accounting courses she took during her two-year attendance at Western Reserve University crucial to launching her career, first as an accountant and later as a stockbroker. Debrah Lee Charatan earned her bachelor's degree by attending college at night. She now looks back at her achievements and confesses that her only regret in starting her own business was that she did not major in business while going to college.

It does not take a genius to observe that a one-person band never gets very big. To conduct a symphony one must let others play. Great conductors always concentrate on conducting, not on playing the various instruments. For that, they find people better at it than they, and assign to them the task of playing those instruments. Following this line of thought, observation and research clearly indicate that successful entrepreneurs who are deficient in certain skills quickly recognize those deficiencies and associate themselves with players more proficient in those skills than they. Nevertheless, as pointed out in the previous chapter, it is apparent that since accounting and finance are the *language* of business the successful entrepreneur must find a way of learning at least the fundamentals of these areas either through the formal process of educational courses or the path of self-learning.

ENERGY LEVEL

Arthur Lipper III, chairman, publisher, and editor in chief of *Venture*, and acknowledged as one of America's prominent gurus of entrepreneurship, describes the entrepreneur as a consummate "early riser." Lipper states: "In a recent survey of a group of successful entrepreneurs, it was found that only 3 percent rose after 8:00 A.M., and the vast majority rose before 7:00 A.M. This is not surprising since most entrepreneurs are people of a high energy level, are achievement-oriented, and love what they are doing. They can't wait for the day to begin. They seem to require less sleep than others and tend to be in good health, perhaps as a result of their high energy levels."[13]

In my interviews with the subjects profiled above, each without exception is an early riser, is usually in her office before anyone else, and seems to enjoy exceptionally good health. Not one appears to be overweight, and most report they indulge in a regular program of exercise. This factor of good health cultivation was best summarized by Geraldine Stutz who at age sixty-five admits to having the "constitution of an ox." She stated: "I've inherited an excellent physical condition and I value it, so I take good care of myself—get lots of sleep, eat the right foods, and do lots of exercising. What you really need in a field of endeavor as pressurized as mine is the blessing of good health."

COURAGE

All of the history of America's most successful enterprises indicate that during their growth, and particularly in the early stages, none have had a complete record of continuous smooth sailing without setbacks. At least, I have yet to discover one. It thus follows that the successful entrepreneur must be a person of unusual courage. We might define courage as the ability to act effectively in the face of danger or difficulty, for it involves both awareness and knowledge of danger. The deep meaning of courage might be that a person can look danger in the eye and not be turned aside by it from doing what he or she thinks should be done.

Courage is rare and elusive. It is hard to appraise and is often confused with self-confidence and sometimes foolhardiness. In starting an enterprise, one must cope periodically with money woes, material shortages, labor difficulties, stiff competition, unreasonable customers, and regulatory agencies with unsympathetic attitudes. Many who fall by the wayside after starting new enterprises give up in the face of these obstacles. The superachieving entrepreneur never gives up. She courageously forges ahead—as did Dorothy Brunson when her successful Harlem dress store was squashed by the opening of a Lane Bryant store next to hers. She licked her wounds and pressed on to another undertaking.

When Lane Nemeth of Discovery Toys suffered a sizeable loss in 1983 and had to contemplate liquidating a $10 million business she had built in six years, she mustered the tremendous courage to carry on, correct her mistakes, eat a lot of crow, and bring the enterprise back to profitability. More than any other element, Nemeth's tremendous courage and commitment to the product and the people she had recruited caused her to refuse to think of anything else but to press on and find a way to save her company. Rose Totino's problem was no less difficult when a faulty marketing strategy nearly drove her business to a point where even her own husband recommended they file for bankruptcy. But Rose was made of more courageous stuff and forged on to find a way out of the mess the business was in, moving forward to build a healthy enterprise that eventually netted her a capital gain in excess of $22 million. Diane Von Furstenberg, following the meteoric success of her entry into the women's dress business with sales mushrooming to $65 million, found herself stuck with a $4 million inventory and an almost fatal cash crunch. She courageously battled her way out of what many saw as an insurmountable problem and, in the process, gained the insight on which her future would depend—not as a manufacturer, but as a designer who could license her name and designs to others more competent than she in assuming all the risks of apparel manufacturing. Today, Von Furstenberg, with a modest design staff and facility, rakes in a handsome income for herself from the royalties derived from sales of hundreds of millions of dollars worth of products that carry her name.

Researching the careers of those entrepreneurs who have displayed outstanding courage in building their enterprises, I recall the ancient Aesop fable of two frogs, hopping gaily through the fields and inadvertently jumping into a tub of milk belonging to a farmer who was milking the cows. One of the frogs, realizing the dire predicament he and his friend were in, abandoned all hope, said farewell to his buddy, and descended to the bottom of the tub where he expired from drowning. His more resourceful companion continued to keep his head above the surface, vigorously pumping his legs up and down in the milk, while he kept telling himself, "There's got to be a way out of this mess." As he continued to think and pump his legs up and down, struggling to keep his head above the surface, the churning effect applied to the milk literally turned it into butter, enabling the persistent frog to jump out of the tub from the butter's firm foundation!

Successful entrepreneurs seem to be like that persistent frog of Aesop's fable written in 600 B.C. They never give up!

LUCK AND OTHER ENVIRONMENTAL INFLUENCES

Writing about entrepreneurial characteristics, Arthur Lipper claims that *luck* tends to play a big role in the life of the successful entrepreneur. He points out that "entrepreneurs are people who feel the need to be in control of their lives and even dislike the very idea of luck."[14] Nevertheless, while entrepreneurs tend to excel at spotting opportunities and capitalizing on them, the luck that plays a role in the entrepreneur's success is usually that of location and timing. This is often referred to as "being on the right street corner at the right time." "Chance associations are part of entrepreneurial luck—a college roommate, a childhood friend, or a chance encounter at a business or social gathering," writes Lipper.

Most of the subjects profiled in this book were able to identify single individuals who made a real difference in their successful careers. For instance, Estée Lauder speaks of her Uncle John Schotz, the immigrant chemist who taught her "worlds of knowledge"—as she expressed it—about the use of oils to cleanse, freshen, and moisten the skin, and thus inspired her future. Faith Popcorn speaks of her former colleague at Grey Advertising who "taught me to keep out of trouble, and encouraged me to start my own business." The late Maxey Jarman picked Geraldine Stutz to preside over the financial mess at Henri Bendel's which he had acquired for Genesco. Jarman's great confidence in Stutz paid off handsomely when, in a reasonably short time, she not only turned Bendel's enormous loss into a profit, but eventually bought the store for herself. Debrah Lee Charatan was a protegé of Pat Fields from whom Charatan learned much about the commercial real estate business. When Fields retired, Charatan was displaced by a man. This perceived bad luck became good luck, for the incident triggered her decision to cast off on her own. The financier Gerald Tsai, whom Muriel Siebert had met quite by chance, gave her the idea of starting her own brokerage firm. Maryles Casto started in the travel agency business because her marriage to Mar Dell Casto disqualified her as a flight attendant with Philippine Airlines. (That was a standard rule of most commercial airlines in the 1970s). Casto promptly got a job in a San Francisco travel agency but found her paycheck lower than that of men in the agency doing the same work as she, so she quit to start her own business. Casto's experience demonstrates the element of being "on the right street corner at the right time," for her entry into commercial travel at a time when new corporations in California's Silicon Valley were popping up like mushrooms gave her the opportunity to capitalize on corporate travel needs that have not stopped growing in that area.

Pamela Scurry's decision to start her own business is attributable to two elements of timing—or perhaps, luck. She was out of a job, and a shop on New York's Madison Avenue just happened to be going out of business. With a $10,000 bank loan and her own entrepreneurial drive, she took the plunge and created a brand-new business and new customers for her unique Wicker Garden retail concept. The factor of timing is dramatic in Rose Totino's remarkably successful pizza business. No one in Minneapolis, and few in America, had even heard of pizzas until the GIs began returning from Europe after World War II. Rose opened her little pizza shop in 1950 with a $1,500 bank loan, and soon had people lined up on the street waiting to buy her little pizzas. Thus began what is today a business of some $200 million in annual sales. Rose Totino was indeed on the right street corner, just at the right time!

As mentioned in the opening pages of this book, I continue to be fascinated by the increasing display of successful entrepreneurship among women. As an educator now, but one who was inspired as a child to follow an entrepreneurial path by my father, and influenced by the many environmental factors of my early upbringing and education, an honest self-analysis suggests that I score in the area of four and five in the personality characteristics of Hisrich and Brush's five-point scale shown at the beginning of this chapter. So do all of the subjects profiled in this book.

This raises the question: Are the personality characteristics of entrepreneurs a matter of inheritance, or can they be cultivated? A discussion of this question properly lies within the realm of the behavioral sciences, but my own observations and research suggest that the characteristics referred to are products of both heredity and environmental influences. Writing about the psyche of the entrepreneur in *The New Times Magazine*, Daniel Goleman states, "It is perhaps paradoxical that, although about four out of ten new businesses are begun by women, female entrepreneurs have been little studied by psychologists. The experts who have gathered what sparse data exists on female entrepreneurs believe that it is situational pressures—such as the lack of opportunity in large corporations or the need to work while raising small children—that drive them to create their own businesses. It is in the talents that lead to success that men and women seem to resemble each other most, while they may differ most in their psychological motives."[15] From all material evidence gathered for this book, I tend to confirm Goleman's analysis.

As every teacher soon learns, the best way for the teacher to learn about any new subject is to be called upon to teach it. The subject of entrepreneurs and entrepreneurship has suddenly come into vogue on college campuses. I introduced a new course, "Entrepreneurship and New Venture Management," at the College of New Rochelle in the spring semester of 1987. One outcome of the course, besides augmenting my own knowledge of the subject, has been the realization of how much more there is to be learned, particularly in the areas concerning entrepreneurship and intrapreneurial women. To this end, we now have recently constructed at the college the H. W. Taylor Institute for Entrepreneurial Studies. Named after my father, the institute will be a center for programs of instruction and further research on questions that concern the practice of entrepreneurship and particularly those questions that relate to women.

Like Mitya in *The Brothers Karamazov*, we want very much an answer to the questions.

NOTES

1. Robert Hisrich and Candida Brush, *The Woman Entrepreneur* (Lexington, Mass.: Lexington Books, 1985).

2. Ibid., p. 26.

3. Ibid., p. 23.

4. Ibid., p. 30.

5. Joseph Schumpeter, *Can Capitalism Survive?* (New York: Harper & Row, 1952), p. 72.

6. Hisrich and Brush, *The Woman Entrepreneur*, p. 4.

7. Peter Drucker, *Innovation and Entrepreneurship* (New York: Harper & Row, 1985), p. 21.

8. Personal interview with the author, June 1987.

9. Arthur Lipper III, *Venture's Guide to Investing in Private Companies* (New York: Dow Jones, Irwin, 1984), Appendix B, p. 179.

10. Charles Garfield, *Peak Performers* (New York: William Morrow & Co., 1986), p. 143.

11. *Venture*, July 1986, p. 35.

12. *Business Week*, June 22, 1987, p. 76.

13. Lipper, *Investing in Private Companies*, p. 9.

14. Ibid., p. 8.

15. Daniel Goleman, "The Psyche of the Entrepreneur," *New York Times Magazine*, February 2, 1986, p. 30.

BIBLIOGRAPHY

Agor, Weston H. *Intuitive Management*. Englewood Cliffs, N.J.: Prentice-Hall, 1984.

Ash, Mary Kay. *Mary Kay*. New York: Harper & Row, 1981.

———. *Mary Kay on People Management*. New York: Warner Books, 1984.

Bastick, Tony. *Intuition: How We Think and Act*. New York: John Wiley & Sons, 1982.

Baumback, Clifford L. *How to Organize and Operate a Small Business*. Englewood Cliffs, N.J.: Prentice-Hall, 1988.

Blotnick, Trully. *Otherwise Engaged: The Private Lives of Successful Career Women*. New York: Penguin Books, 1985.

Brandt, Steven C. *Entrepreneuring—10 Commandments for Building a Growth Company*. Reading, Mass.: Addison-Wesley, 1982.

Drucker, Peter. *Innovation and Entrepreneurship*. New York: Harper & Row, 1985.

———. *Management*. New York: Harper & Row, 1974.

Easton, T. A., and Conant, R. W. *Cutting Loose: Making the Transition from Employee to Entrepreneur*. Chicago: Probus Publishing Co., 1985.

Fritz, Roger. *Nobody Gets Rich by Working for Someone Else—An Entrepreneur's Guide*. New York: Dodd, Mead & Co., 1987.

Garfield, Charles. *Peak Performers*. New York: William Morrow & Co., 1986.

Greenfield, W. M. *Calculated Risk: A Guide to Entrepreneurship*. Lexington, Mass.: D. C. Heath & Co., 1986.

Henderson, James W. *Obtaining Venture Financing*. Lexington, Mass.: Lexington Books, 1987.

Hisrich, Robert D. *Entrepreneurship, Intrapreneurship and Venture Capital.* Lexington, Mass.: Lexington Books, 1986.

Hisrich, Robert D., and Brush, Candida G. *The Woman Entrepreneur.* Lexington, Mass.: Lexington Books, 1985.

Israel, Lee. *Estée Lauder: Beyond the Magic.* Englewood Cliffs, N.J.: Prentice-Hall, 1984.

Kent, C. A., Sexton, D. L., and Vesper, K. H., eds. *Encyclopedia of Entrepreneurship.* Englewood Cliffs, N.J.: Prentice-Hall, 1982.

Lauder, Estée. *Estée: A Success Story.* New York: Random House, 1985.

Levitt, Theodore. *The Marketing Imagination.* New York: The Free Press, 1983.

Lipper, Arthur, III, *Venture's Guide to Investing in Private Companies.* Homewood, Ill.: Dow Jones Irwin, 1984.

Mancuso, J. R. *How to Start, Finance, and Manage Your Own Small Business.* Englewood Cliffs, N.J.: Prentice-Hall, 1984.

McQuown, Judith H. *Inc. Yourself.* New York: Warner Books, 1984.

Nelton, Sharon. *In Love and In Business.* New York: John Wiley & Sons, 1986.

Pine, Carol, and Mundale, Susan. *Self-Made.* Minneapolis, Minn.: Dorn Books, 1982.

Pinchot, Gifford. *Intrapreneuring: Why You Don't Have to Leave the Corporation to Become an Entrepreneur.* New York: Harper & Row, 1985.

Rowan, Roy. *The Intuitive Manager.* Boston: Little, Brown & Co., 1986.

Sargent, A. E. *The Androgynous Manager.* New York: Amacon, 1981.

Schumpeter, Joseph. *Can Capitalism Survive?* New York: Harper & Row, 1952.

Scollard, Jeanette R. *The Self-Employed Woman.* New York: Simon & Schuster, 1985.

Sexton, D. L., and Smilor, R. W. *The Art and Science of Entrepreneurship.* Cambridge, Mass.: Ballinger Publishing, 1986.

Sheehy, Gail. *Passages.* New York: E. P. Dutton, 1974.

Sobel, Robert, and Sicilian, David. *The Entrepreneurs.* Boston: Houghton Mifflin, 1986.

Tepper, Terri P., and Tepper, Nona D. *The New Entrepreneurs—Women Working from Home.* New York: Universe Books, 1980.

INDEX

About the Author

RUSSEL R. TAYLOR is Chairman of the Business Department and founder and director of the H.W. Taylor Institute for Entrepreneurial Studies at the College of New Rochelle.